Praise for

You're Grown–
NOW YOU CAN THROW A PARTY

"Nothing's more fun than partying with Sallie! A fearless and creative cook, Sallie is a passionate teacher with a nurturing nature, the result of many years of counseling young people. But mostly, it is her clever, artistic touches, and her ability to elevate the everyday into something special that makes her one of the most gifted party givers I know. Here is a great book full of fun recipes and party ideas for the young and the young at heart!"

—EMILY FRITH, Well known Nashville chef, caterer, owner of Nashville's Corner Market, and Food Network Contestant

Happy cooking!
Happy parties!
Sallie Swor

You're Grown–
NOW YOU CAN THROW A PARTY

Sallie Stamps Swor

You're Grown—Now You Can Throw A Party

by Sallie Stamps Swor

© Copyright 2017 Sallie Stamps Swor

ISBN 978-1-63393-478-8

Published by

 köehlerbooks™

210 60th Street
Virginia Beach, VA 23451
800-435-4811
www.koehlerbooks.com

DEDICATION

For my son Richard, who makes every day a party, and my husband, Sammy, who keeps the party going. To all my family and friends who make party-giving worthwhile. To my mother, who just threw herself a 90th birthday party, I couldn't ask for more inspiration. To my sister and my best friends, who let me cook the same dish over and over and then take pictures, and still enjoy every bite with enthusiasm. To all of you—the knitters, the gardeners, the readers, the cooks, and the kind friends and family who have encouraged me along the way. You know who you are, and you know that you're the reason I continue to "Throw a Party."

And finally, we all know that no one really cooks alone. We are surrounded by generations of cooks from our past, and we keep our guests and family constantly in our minds. Whether I'm recreating a recipe from my grandmother's collection or planning a menu to please friends, these are the reasons my kitchen is always full and always ready for that party to begin.

Table of Contents

About the Cookbook

This cookbook, *You're Grown—Now You Can Throw a Party*, is designed for anyone who not only wants to cook, but also wants to cook for friends and would like to entertain by hosting parties. Why do you want to throw a party? Simple answer—to have a good time, and to celebrate with your friends and your family. It really is fun to make good food and share it with your friends. Every recipe in this book has been tried time and again, and they have all proven to be favorites. Whether you are hosting a cocktail party for twenty friends, a seated dinner for six, a surprise birthday bash, a picnic on the porch, or an impromptu Saturday brunch, you will find the perfect menus and ideas in this book. Hosting will never seem overwhelming with these recipes at hand. If you serve good food and you have a good time, then everyone will be delighted. I have a friend who always says, "I'm just so thrilled to be invited." That's how your party guests will feel.

You're Grown—Now You Can Throw a Party encourages friends and family to cook together and enjoy entertaining. I tell people all the time that I'm not a trained chef, so all of the recipes I use have to be easy to create in a simple home kitchen. This book is for people who would love to have parties and provide delicious food made from simple directions explaining exactly what you need to know about each recipe: the ingredients and where to get them, the cooking equipment required, and exactly what to do in easy-to-read, step-by-step instructions. This book is for anyone, from a novice chef to a seasoned cook, who wants to entertain and doesn't have hours of time to spend in the kitchen. Many of these recipes take only minutes to prepare, and others can be prepared ahead of time. This is a collection of recipes and tips to keep entertaining simple enough that the host will also most definitely enjoy throwing a party.

You're Grown—Now You Can Throw a Party contains a feast of possibilities for creating menus, designing simple table settings, and pre-planning almost any occasion. The sources and suggestions are both practical and accessible. Menu planning and party ideas are included, presented with entertaining and informative text to make this cookbook a joy to read. Impromptu parties are encouraged, and anyone can always find quick, reliable, and fun suggestions for menus to create with confidence in this book. The end results will always be delicious, and compliments are a guarantee. The best parties are the ones where the hosts are having as much fun as the guests. Now you can throw a party and have fun too! Cooking for anyone is truly a gift of love. These are the recipes that will become the favorites you'll be serving to friends and family for the rest of your life!

1
One Well-Stocked Kitchen and Bar

THE KITCHEN

It all begins with a well-stocked kitchen, the backbone of any home. People frequently ask what is in a well-stocked kitchen and the answer is easy—the things you use most. My first apartment was roughly the size of a one-car garage. I made shelves out of crates since there wasn't a pantry. I kept olive oil, canned tomatoes, pasta, rice, grits (I'm Southern), dried beans, canned soups, and basic baking supplies, plus a shoebox with dried herbs and spices on those shelves. The waist-high fridge always had butter, milk, eggs, cheese, assorted condiments, and maybe wine. The point is to designate a place—no matter how tiny—to keep what you need. That's how I started cooking and throwing parties, and this method taught me to ask questions about every recipe I make.

1. Can I get the ingredients at almost any grocery store?
2. Can I substitute something for an ingredient if I don't have it?
3. Can I make this without a lot of equipment and weird techniques?
4. Will the ingredients be practical to use again?

If the answer to all four was yes, then I gave the recipe a shot. I'm still doing that. I've made "use what you have" my personal motto when following a recipe. It would be terrible to think that being one garlic clove short of a recipe's ingredient list would keep someone from making dinner!

Stocking a kitchen is basic, but also personal. If you like tuna, keep it on hand; if you use a lot of Indian spices, add those to your spice cabinet.

This is the list we've used to stock several kitchens as my son moved into new apartments. It reflects a couple of additions he found necessary after cooking more often. We personalized the list by adding favorites, like orange juice, deli meats, ground beef, and ice cream. Start a wish list for some appliances you would like to add. We also scoured Goodwill and thrift shops for an iron skillet and some great casserole dishes. Use this list as a starting point, and then make it your own. Happy cooking!

- **Pots and Pans:** 2 non-stick skillets (small and large), small and large saucepans with lids, Dutch oven, baking sheet, pie pan, 2 cake pans, 2 casserole dishes (9 x 13 and 8 x 8), bread pan, set of mixing bowls
- **Utensils:** small and large spatulas, plastic flexible spatula, tongs, 2 large spoons for stirring (slotted spoon and wooden spoon), whisk, cheese grater (can also be used to zest lemons), 3 good knives (small, medium, and large), serrated knife, set of measuring cups, measuring spoons, cutting board, colander, vegetable peeler, can opener, hot pads, rolling pin
- **Small Appliances:** mixer (stand or hand-held), blender, coffee pot (if you are a coffee drinker), microwave, slow cooker, and definitely put a food processor on the wish list
- **Staples for Cooking:** salt, kosher salt, pepper (a pepper grinder is also nice to own), flour, cornmeal, sugar, brown sugar, maple syrup, powdered sugar, honey, baking soda, baking powder, olive oil, canola oil, cooking spray, hot sauce, soy sauce, vinegars (apple cider and balsamic), bouillon cubes (beef, chicken, and vegetable), cocoa powder, chocolate chips, vanilla extract, nuts, Ramen noodles, rice, dried beans, pasta, quinoa, oatmeal, dry cereal, popcorn, coffee, tea
- **12 Essential Spices:** basil, chili powder, cinnamon, cumin, curry powder, nutmeg, oregano, paprika, red pepper flakes, rosemary, sage, thyme, garlic salt (not really a spice, but very useful)
- **Refrigerator:** butter (salted and/or unsalted), milk, eggs, bread, mayonnaise, mustard, ketchup, salsa, pickles, sour cream, jelly or jam, yogurt, cheeses of choice, proteins of choice
- **Fruit and Veggie Drawer of Refrigerator:** potatoes, onions, carrots, apples and other fruits, lemons, spinach, lettuce, plus other vegetables you like
- **Freezer:** frozen vegetables, frozen fruit, chicken breasts, frozen yogurt or ice cream, plus foods you like for convenience
- **Storage and Cooking:** plastic wrap, resealable baggies (large and small), waxed paper, aluminum foil, plastic containers, parchment paper

THE BAR

For anyone who enjoys throwing a party, a well-stocked bar is certainly an asset. But the answer to what is in a well-stocked bar, just like with a kitchen, is to stock it with the spirits you like best. Although I've recently acquired a small bar area in my house, for years we just had a cabinet where we kept liquor, and for parties I put whatever I thought was necessary on a tray on the kitchen counter. Some people stock a bar with tons of varieties of fancy names and brands, but I think you can be an excellent host and still start small with just the basics. There is no point in cluttering your bar with obscure liquors you'll never use. You can always add to your bar over time. In fact, most alcohol keeps for a very long time. It's always entertaining to have a signature cocktail for a party, but it's nice to let your company mix their own drinks too. Fancy glassware and bar tools are great to collect but not necessary as long as you have a corkscrew, a bottle opener, a jigger, and some glasses.

Basic go-to staples are wine (red and white), beer, gin, vodka, bourbon, scotch, tequila, and rum. After that you can add anything you like according to taste preferences. I like to have orange liqueur, vermouth, amaretto, and cognac on hand. Good mixers are tonic, club soda, cola, and fruit juices. Do make sure to have plenty of ice, and keep some non-alcoholic choices on hand for friends who don't drink alcohol. The choices are endless, but this is a good starting place should you decide to stock your own bar.

II
Two Late-Night Suppers

When I was in college I worked in restaurants, sometimes until late at night. Afterward I was always starving, and so I picked up a few tricks for quick but satisfying late-night suppers. I hope you'll have some excellent reasons for a late-night supper; for example, you've just returned home after seeing a fabulous play, and your date is looking at you with "hungry eyes"—well maybe not you, but your refrigerator. Instead of standing in front of the fridge waiting for something marvelous to appear, you can delight your guest with either of these two quick but satisfying late-night meals. Neither recipe takes more than 15 minutes to prepare. The **Bonus Recipe: Spinach and Artichoke Heart Salad** is delicious with both dishes. Pour a glass of wine and show off your amazing culinary skills. Either recipe is also perfect for an impromptu party or a satisfying supper. Or treat yourself. Enjoying a fine dish is always appropriate!

Crispy Skillet Pizza

INGREDIENTS

1 tsp olive oil

8-inch flour tortilla

¼ cup pizza sauce

¼ cup mozzarella cheese, grated

8 to 10 slices pepperoni (or use what you have—leftover chicken, mushrooms, ham)

1 Tbsp Parmesan cheese, grated

Red pepper flakes to taste

DIRECTIONS

Preheat the oven to broil.

Heat an iron skillet or non-stick ovenproof skillet over high heat.

Add olive oil and swirl to coat.

Add flour tortilla to the skillet and cook for 30 seconds to 1 minute to lightly brown the bottom.

Flip tortilla so browned side is up, and remove skillet from heat.

Top the tortilla with a thin layer of pizza sauce, spreading all the way to the edge.

(hint: For crispy edges, let sauce and cheese spread slightly over the sides of the tortilla.)

Top the sauce with mozzarella cheese.

Put pepperoni on top of the cheese and sprinkle with Parmesan and red pepper flakes.

Place the skillet in the oven and broil for 4 to 5 minutes to slightly brown the top.

Remove skillet from the oven, put pizza on a cutting board, and cut into slices.

Serving Suggestion: Top pizza according to your personal taste; try barbeque sauce and cooked chicken, or taco sauce and ground beef, or Alfredo sauce and cooked salmon or shrimp. A few basil or arugula leaves sprinkled on top of a cooked pizza add a little finesse. (hint: A vegetarian pizza is also an easy option. The sky is the limit!)

Serves 1 to 2

Spaghetti alla Carbonara

INGREDIENTS

8 oz dry spaghetti or fettuccini

2 eggs

4 oz bacon or pancetta, cut in 1-inch pieces

¼ cup Parmesan cheese, grated

¼ cup pecorino cheese, grated
(or use another ¼ cup Parmesan)

¼ tsp black pepper

¼ tsp salt

DIRECTIONS

In a large pot, bring about 6 cups water with 1 Tbsp salt to a boil.

Add the spaghetti and cook for 8 to 10 minutes or until al dente according to package directions.

Drain pasta, reserving ½ cup of the cooking water.

While the pasta is cooking, heat a large skillet over medium high heat.

Add bacon or pancetta and sauté for 3 to 4 minutes until the meat is crispy.

Remove bacon or pancetta to drain on paper towels, and remove skillet from heat.

In a small bowl, whisk the eggs, cheese, salt, and pepper until well combined.

Return the skillet to heat, and add half of the reserved pasta water.

Toss in the spaghetti and shake the skillet over the heat for a few seconds until the bubbling stops.

Remove the skillet from heat and add the egg mixture, stirring quickly until the mixture thickens.

Stir in bacon or pancetta.

Season liberally with black pepper.

Divide the pasta into bowls and serve immediately with extra cheese for topping.

Serves 2

Make It an Occasion:

The simplest salad I make with the biggest compliment factor is **Bonus Recipe: Spinach and Artichoke Heart Salad** *(pg. 11)*. Bagged spinach keeps for several days, making it a good thing to have in the fridge, and I always keep a can or two of good quality artichoke hearts packed in water in the pantry. Even a late-night supper deserves to be served with some soft music and maybe candlelight.

Combine half a bag of spinach leaves with 4 drained and rinsed artichoke hearts, cut in bite sized pieces.

Dressing: In a jar combine 2 Tbsp flavored balsamic vinegar (lemon is a favorite) with 2 Tbsp olive oil, 1 clove garlic, minced, ½ tsp salt, ¼ tsp pepper, and 2 tsp sugar. Shake it up and pour over the salad.

Serves 2

III
Three Classic Cocktails with a Snack

Drink menus at fancy bars are currently quite the thing, as each venue tries to outdo the next with the most amazing concoctions. Sometimes I get so involved in reading the menus that I almost forget to order. Almost. Cocktails can be a lot of fun, but if the list of different alcohols in one is as long as the page, I'm not going to be re-creating it at home. In fact, it sounds like it's better to just ignore it altogether.

Your best bet is to have a few basic cocktails that you can rely on for entertaining and that do not require you to seek a loan to purchase the ingredients. The three here—**Bloody Mary**, **Kir Royale**, and **Mint Julep**—are easy to master and sure to delight. They are each paired with a perfect snack, so you can plan an easy get-together with a few friends at home. Your guests will not miss the bar snacks or prices. Throughout this cookbook you will find several delicious cocktail recipes suggested with different menus. Try them all and find your favorites. Suggestions for planning and hosting a cocktail party are on page 117.

For friends who do not drink alcohol, remember to keep ingredients for "Mocktails"—plenty of fruit juice and sparkling water, soft drinks and flavored waters. And those **Tiny Cheese Biscuits** *(pg. 18)*—I promise you'll be very glad to have that recipe.

Caroline's Bloody Mary, Simple Homemade Sausage (pg. 46), and Buttermilk Biscuits (pg. 54)

A Bloody Mary, and Garlic and Curry Candied Pecans

A Bloody Mary often tastes better before a meal, because it's so flavorful on its own. But I do like a Bloody Mary served with a little snack that's both salty and sweet like these **Garlic and Curry Candied Pecans**. They are always a hit. Keep these pecans on hand for snacking. Of course, you can buy prepared Bloody Mary mixes, but this recipe has a lovely fresh taste.

Caroline's Bloody Mary

INGREDIENTS

1½ oz vodka	1 tsp Worcestershire sauce	½ tsp prepared horseradish
3 oz tomato juice	3 or 4 drops hot sauce	Pinch salt (I like garlic salt)
Juice of ½ a lemon	¼ tsp celery salt	2 tsp dill pickle juice

DIRECTIONS

For each cocktail, fill tall glasses with ice. Combine ingredients and pour over ice in glass. (*hint: You can make the recipe for more than one cocktail in a pitcher and pour drinks remembering to stir before each pour so ingredients are well combined.*)

Optional garnishes: celery, olives, **Bonus Recipe: Pickled Okra**

We grow okra and hot peppers so this is a tradition. Divide 2 lb washed okra pods, 4 peeled garlic cloves, 2 seeded thin sliced jalapenos, and 4 sprigs of fresh dill between 4 pint-sized clean canning jars. Bring to a boil: 2 cups water, 2 cups rice vinegar or white vinegar, ¼ cup salt, 1 Tbsp mustard seed. Ladle hot vinegar liquid over okra mixture leaving about ½ inch space at the top. Cover with lids. Cool and store in the fridge for up to 3 months. Makes a great gift, just add a label and a bow!

Garlic and Curry Candied Pecans

INGREDIENTS

1 lb pecans	1½ tsp garlic salt
1 egg white	1½ tsp salt (coarse or flakey salt is nice)
¾ cup sugar	⅛ tsp cayenne pepper
1 tsp curry powder	

DIRECTIONS

Preheat the oven to 250 degrees.

Line a cookie sheet with foil, and spray with cooking spray.

Spread pecans on the cookie sheet and toast for 10 minutes.

In a large bowl, whisk egg white with 1 tsp of water until frothy.

Mix in seasonings and sugar.

Add pecans, stirring to coat them thoroughly.

Return to cookie sheet and bake for 1 hour until pecans are dry, stirring twice.

Cool and store in an airtight container.

Serving Suggestion: These pecans are an excellent hostess or holiday gift. Pack in a pretty container.

A Kir Royale and Tiny Cheese Biscuits

An elegant cocktail deserves an elegant snack.

Kir Royale

INGREDIENTS

    6 oz sparkling wine

    ½ oz crème de cassis (can substitute raspberry liqueur)

    Lemon peel for garnish

DIRECTIONS

    For each cocktail, pour sparkling wine in a champagne glass, top with crème de cassis and garnish with a lemon peel.

Tiny Cheese Biscuits

You will be stunned, shocked, amazed, and mostly thrilled. These are the most delicious little morsels you will ever taste, and they only have *three ingredients*! Cut them out with a smaller biscuit cutter and they are adorable. It's been my secret for years—now you have it!

INGREDIENTS

1 (8-oz) package cream cheese

10 Tbsp butter (1 stick plus 2 Tbsp)

1 cup self-rising flour (see pg. 54 to make this flour if you don't have any)

DIRECTIONS

Combine all ingredients in a food processor and pulse until a ball of dough starts to form (can be done with an electric mixer or by hand).

Pat dough into a disk and wrap in plastic wrap.

Refrigerate for an hour (up to four hours).

Preheat the oven to 425 degrees.

Line a baking sheet with parchment paper, or spray with cooking spray.

Roll out dough on a floured surface, lightly flouring the top of the dough, to about ¼-inch thick (use waxed paper for an easy cleanup).

Cut biscuits with a small cutter and space about an inch apart on the baking sheet.

Re-roll remaining dough to cut as many biscuits as possible.

Bake about 12 minutes or until tops are lightly brown.

Best when warm, so enjoy right now!

The size of the biscuit cutter determines the quantity.

A Mint Julep with Country Ham Salad Sandwiches

They're not just for Derby Day. Mint Juleps are refreshing and festive. Surprise your guests with this classic combo of a Mint Julep and a **Country Ham Salad Sandwich**. This is an old-fashioned sandwich spread and a most requested recipe.

Richard's Mint Julep

INGREDIENTS
Bourbon

Crushed ice

Mint leaves, plus sprigs for garnish

Simple syrup (recipe follows)

DIRECTIONS
Make simple syrup by bringing 2 cups of water and 2 cups of sugar to a boil.

Add one mint sprig to the simple syrup as it cools.

For each cocktail fill a julep or similar size cocktail glass with ice.

Add 1½ oz bourbon and fill the rest of the glass with cooled simple syrup. Garnish with a mint sprig. *(hint: I like a little club soda in mine!)*

Country Ham Salad (pg. 21) in Beaten Biscuits (from You're Grown blog, TheDeerOne.com/recipes)

Country Ham Salad Sandwiches

INGREDIENTS

16 oz country ham slices (can substitute 4 to 6 oz of country ham for the same amount of regular "city" ham if you want to cut back on saltiness)

1 clove garlic, peeled (or very small amount of onion)

6 Tbsp butter, cut in pieces

2 Tbsp sweet pickle juice

5 or 6 sweet pickles

Thin-sliced bread

DIRECTIONS

Cook country ham until extra crispy. *(hint: Can be done in a skillet or in the oven on a foil-lined sheet at 375 degrees. Baking takes about 10 to 15 minutes and keeps grease to a minimum, making cleanup easier.)*

Add cooled ham slices and garlic to the food processor, and pulse to grind.

Add butter, pickle juice, and pickles, and pulse until finely ground and mixture holds together (add more butter if necessary).

Spread on slices of thin bread, top with another bread slice, and cut into triangles or desired shapes.

Makes 12 whole sandwiches

Serving Suggestion: Great in **Beaten Biscuits**, recipe in "You're Grown" blog—it's a Southern classic. TheDeerOne.com/recipes

IV
Four Favorite Picnics

Once, I heard someone say they hated picnics, and my first thought was that they must not be doing it right. If you have to work too hard, then it's not a picnic (at least not for you). Here's the thing—lugging baskets and coolers and blankets all over the place to find a perfect spot isn't all that much fun. Really, any picnic should be approached with a sort of "devil may care" attitude. Accept the facts; you don't control the temperature, the bugs, the pollen, or the wind. But you can control the food, the company, and the attitude! That's a perfect excuse for a make-ahead **Barbeque Picnic** *(pg. 24)*

I am a picnic-loving girl. When I was little, my family turned any nice day into a picnic. We had an old-fashioned picnic table in our back yard that backed up to a creek, which occasionally ran after a good rain. Any notion that a picnic had to have a theme and fancy food was completely destroyed by the time I was old enough to plan my own picnics. In fact, in college, my friends and I took our cafeteria lunch and a blanket to our dorm roof to enjoy a picnic. (Not as daring as it sounds—the roof was flat.)

By definition, a picnic is eating good food in a pretty place with people you like. My son loves a nice rainy-day front-porch picnic. His menu will always involve **Sallie's Sort of Pimento Cheese** *(pg. 40)* in a sandwich. I like to carry a picnic blanket down to the creek on pretty days, sip **Chilled Avocado Soup** *(pg. 31)*, and lie around in the sun with a good friend or a good book or both. For a bigger group, we might pack up a cooler with **Bruschetta and Toppings** *(pg. 26)* and head for a pool. There are so many reasons for a picnic: tailgating, driving to the lake for a day, enjoying the garden, sitting by a pool, lounging on a screened in porch, going to the park, skipping a day at work—see what I mean? Once you get the hang of it, you'll find a million reasons to picnic. Here are some excellent recipes to help. Mix and match, adding in store-bought items you like. Let your motto be "Life is a Picnic." Now you're doing it right.

WHAT TO BRING BESIDES THE FOOD AND BEVERAGES

Bug spray, sunscreen, trash bags, water, paper towels, and damp wipes are always a good idea. Blankets are required equipment if you are going somewhere without picnic tables. A roll of craft paper and a box of crayons can turn a boring park picnic table into a work of art, plus provide hours of entertainment. Plates, napkins, utensils, and ice are essential. Salt and pepper are nice to include. A corkscrew and bottle opener can save the day. The rest depends on what you pack for your picnic. Have fun!

A Barbeque Picnic

A perfect barbeque picnic is one where you, as host, are not sweating over a hot grill while everyone else is drinking your beer and having a good time. The perfect barbeque picnic is one that you make ahead of time. The barbeque can be wrapped and toted to any location, or it can be served on a screened-in porch, by a pool, or right in your own back yard. What seems like hours of work is actually only a bit of pre-planning and minutes of prep. The grill and oven do your work. The grocery store has your back.

Barbeque Turkey Breast

INGREDIENTS

3 to 5 lb turkey breast (easier to find frozen), defrosted, rinsed, and dried

3 Tbsp paprika

3 Tbsp brown sugar

2 Tbsp garlic salt

¼ tsp cayenne pepper

1 Tbsp liquid smoke (It sounds weird, but it gives meat a smoky flavor—a little goes a long way.)

Barbeque Sauce

1 cup apple cider vinegar	1 tsp salt
1¼ cups ketchup	Hot sauce to taste
1¼ cups brown sugar	

DIRECTIONS

Light the grill or heat broiler to high heat.

Combine paprika, brown sugar, garlic salt, and cayenne pepper, and rub over turkey breast.

Grill or broil each side of the turkey breast until it begins to brown.

Preheat the oven to 300 degrees.

Line a baking pan with heavy aluminum foil.

Place turkey breast on foil and pour liquid smoke over the top.

Cover the turkey breast with foil and seal completely.

Bake 3 to 3½ hours.

Allow meat to cool enough to shred.

For sauce, combine all sauce ingredients in a saucepan and bring to a boil.

Cool and store in a jar.

To serve, place shredded turkey in an ovenproof casserole or disposable foil pan. Mix in half of the sauce, save the rest for your picnic, and reheat the barbeque. It will stay warm for at least an hour wrapped in foil or covered. *(hint: Broil shredded turkey for additional crispy pieces.)*

Serve on buns or rolls or with **Sweet Jalapeño Cornbread** *(pg. 100)*.

Serves 10

Note: Turkey and sauce can be prepared a day ahead and kept refrigerated.

Make It a Picnic

Pack barbeque in a covered dish or aluminum foil pan wrapped in foil. Add **Swor House Baked Beans** *(pg. 114)* to the menu, also prepared in an ovenproof dish or aluminum foil pan, and stir up a pre-packed coleslaw mix for a quick side. Pick up rolls or buns at the grocery store. Tell your best friend to bring the **Stuffed Eggs** *(pg. 130)*. You might even make a batch of **Firecrackers** *(pg. 121)* to enjoy before the real feasting begins. Now what to drink? Local beer is great with barbeque. Use paper plates and plastic silverware for easy cleanup. I'm not totally sure, but paper towels seem like appropriate napkins for a barbeque. Now relax and enjoy!

A Bruschetta Picnic

This is an absolutely genius way to host a picnic and please every single guest. A Bruschetta Picnic doesn't have to celebrate any particular occasion and it doesn't require much work. A little organizing and you've got a picnic going. Toast the bruschetta and provide a variety of your favorite mix and match toppings, from sweet to savory. Guests serve themselves. It's an event in itself just to see what everybody creates. Plus, bruschetta is truly finger food, kind of like little plates—maybe a bit messier, but hey, it's a picnic, and mess isn't a problem when you're having that much fun. Remember that bruschetta makes a great appetizer too.

Bruschetta

DIRECTIONS

Preheat the oven to 350 degrees.*

Cut a baguette into diagonal slices about ¾ of an inch thick.

Brush baguette slices on both sides with olive oil, and lightly season with salt.

Place on a baking sheet (line with foil for easy cleanup) and bake, turning over once, until golden, 10 to 12 minutes. Cool.

*If you would like to grill the bruschetta, heat the grill until really hot, and place slices of baguette—brushed with oil and sprinkled with salt—on the grill, turning once about a minute per side or until grill marks appear.

For a picnic count on at least 4 to 6 bruschetta for each person.

Toppings

This part is a breeze. Many toppings can be purchased, and some ideas follow these four recipes for classic toppings that you can prepare ahead of time. If you only make one, the **Tomato Topping** is the most traditional, but all four are especially easy and delicious. The **Artichoke Heart and Parmesan Topping** is like a mini Caesar salad on toast!

Tomato Topping for Bruschetta

INGREDIENTS

2 pints cherry or grape tomatoes, cut in half (a mix of red and yellow is pretty)

3 to 4 cloves of garlic, finely minced

10 to 15 basil leaves, cut in thin slices (chiffonade)

1 Tbsp balsamic vinegar

1 Tbsp olive oil

½ tsp salt

¼ tsp red pepper flakes

DIRECTIONS

Combine all ingredients. Keep at room temperature.

Artichoke Heart and Parmesan Topping for Bruschetta

INGREDIENTS

2 jars marinated artichoke hearts, drained and chopped

2 Tbsp parsley, minced

½ cup Parmesan cheese, grated

2 Tbsp olive oil

1 clove garlic, minced

Salt and pepper to taste

DIRECTIONS

Combine all ingredients.

Arugula Tuna and White Bean Topping for Bruschetta

INGREDIENTS

1 cup roughly chopped arugula leaves

1 can tuna, well drained (or 4 to 5 oz leftover flaked *Seared Tuna pg. 147)*

1 can white beans, drained and rinsed

1 clove garlic, finely minced

¼ tsp red pepper flakes

1 Tbsp red wine vinegar

3 Tbsp olive oil

Salt and pepper to taste (tuna and canned beans have different salt levels)

DIRECTIONS

Combine all ingredients.

Honey Balsamic Strawberry Topping for Bruschetta

INGREDIENTS

1 pint strawberries, sliced

10 fresh basil leaves, thinly sliced (chiffonade)

4 oz feta or goat cheese, crumbled

1 Tbsp balsamic vinegar

2 Tbsp honey

DIRECTIONS

Combine all ingredients.

Possibilities for Purchase

Cheese: Try a couple of different cheeses for a picnic, like ricotta, brie, mozzarella, Parmesan, mascarpone, burrata, or any other favorite.

Deli: Add hard salami, prosciutto, ham, or smoked salmon.

Spreads: Try pesto or olive tapenade.

Fruits and Veggies: Choose anything, just be sure to slice ahead of time. I like bell peppers, onions, radishes, melons, grapes, and pears. *(hint: If little ones are invited, peanut butter and bananas are not a bad idea.)*

Serving Suggestion: *The Sandwich fillings (pg. 37)* will all work as toppings as well.

Make It a Picnic

This picnic is very easy to pack up and take anywhere. Use disposable plastic containers and paper plates and, for a cute party idea, wrap plastic silverware in bandanas to use as napkins—they usually cost less than a dollar at discount stores or online. Pick two or three toppings to make and a few to purchase. Prepare the bruschetta ahead of time and pack the toppings separately. Everyone can serve themselves, even if they mess up your perfect combinations by, say, serving brie with pesto! This is a complete menu with appetizers, main course, and dessert. Anyone for **Bonus Recipe: Rosé Spritzer** *(pg. 40)*? PS: don't forget trash bags and a corkscrew!

Chilled Soups for Picnics

You can pour these soups into small mason jars for individual servings and tie a plastic spoon to each jar with a piece of twine or ribbon, or pour soups into a thermos and bring along paper cups. Cold soup at a picnic is such a treat. But remember, cold soups aren't just for picnics. They can be an elegant start to any dinner.

Gazpacho

My good friend Jim made the first gazpacho I ever tasted. It was love at first slurp.

INGREDIENTS

3 or 4 tomatoes, cut in quarters

2 cloves garlic, peeled

1 onion, peeled and quartered

1 cucumber, peeled and cut in several pieces

1 red pepper (or green or yellow pepper), seeded and quartered

1 tsp oregano

1 tsp salt

1 tsp sugar

3 Tbsp red wine vinegar

1 Tbsp olive oil

¼ cup water or a small can of tomato juice

Optional: several drops of hot sauce

DIRECTIONS

Combine all ingredients in the blender and blend to desired consistency; we like a few vegetables still chunky.

Chill until very cold.

Serves 8

Chilled Avocado Soup

One of my college professors invited our class over for a picnic and made avocado soup. I thought it was the most exotic thing in the world. Maybe it is!

INGREDIENTS

3 avocados, peeled, pit removed

1½ cups chicken or vegetable broth

⅓ cup heavy cream

1 Tbsp lemon juice

Salt to taste (broth can be salty—I like a tiny pinch of garlic salt)

DIRECTIONS

Combine all ingredients in blender. Serve very cold.

Serves 8

Serving Suggestion: I have served this topped with crabmeat and finely chopped tomatoes. Heavenly!

Cold Curried Squash Soup

INGREDIENTS

3 large yellow squash, chopped	1 tsp sugar
1 onion, chopped	1 Tbsp lemon juice
1 tsp curry powder	¼ cup heavy cream
3 Tbsp butter	½ tsp pepper
4 cups chicken or vegetable broth	Salt to taste (broth can be salty)

DIRECTIONS

Melt butter in a Dutch oven or large pot over medium high heat.

Add squash and onion, and sauté about 5 minutes until they are soft.

Stir in curry powder and cook another minute.

Add broth, reduce heat, and let soup simmer about 20 minutes.

Allow soup to cool enough to purée in the blender, adding cream and lemon juice.

Add salt if needed.

Serve cold.

Serves 8

Vichyssoise

My mom and her friends cherished a recipe for **Vichyssoise** made with canned potato soup. It was what I grew up with. Then I had the real stuff and I was hooked. I thought it must be too hard to make. I experimented, and guess what—it's not. It's easy as can be. You do have to peel two potatoes, but it's worth it.

INGREDIENTS

2 Tbsp butter

2 large baking potatoes, peeled and cubed

2 or 3 leeks washed and trimmed, white part only, or 1 large onion, peeled and chopped

5 cups stock, chicken or vegetable

1 cup heavy cream

1 Tbsp chives or green onion, finely chopped

1 tsp salt, more to taste (stock has different levels of salt)

Optional: extra chives or thinly sliced green onions to garnish

DIRECTIONS

Melt butter in a Dutch oven or large pot over medium high heat.

Add potatoes and leeks or onions and cook for 2 or 3 minutes until they begin to soften.

Add broth and simmer until potatoes are falling-apart tender, about 20 minutes.

Allow soup to cool enough to blend in a blender.

Add cream and chives to blended soup, taste for salt, and refrigerate until serving time.

Serve chilled, topped with extra chives if desired.

This is even better if you have time to make it the day before.

Serves 8

Champagne and Peach Soup

Who says it has to be difficult to be delicious? And yes, sparkling wine and prosecco are not real champagne, but doesn't it sound better? Sort of like saying escargot instead of snails?

INGREDIENTS

    1 quart really good peach ice cream, slightly melted

    12 oz sparkling wine (prosecco, cava, or champagne)

    Mint leaves make a nice garnish.

DIRECTIONS

    Combine ingredients and serve chilled topped with a mint leaf if desired.

    Serves 12

Make It a Picnic

Pick one of these delicious soups and pair it with two different sandwiches from *The Sandwiches (pg. 37)*. If you are traveling with your picnic to a selected setting, as opposed to walking a short distance, like to your porch, put your soup in a freezable container and allow it to almost freeze. It will help keep food in your cooler cold. Here is another idea—have a cold soup picnic. Pack 2 or 3 soups; bring paper cups and spoons, plus a plate of your favorite cheeses and crackers. That can be done ahead of time to keep it easy. Did I mention that **Champagne and Peach Soup** makes a lovely dessert?

Country Ham Salad Sandwiches (pg. 21),
Sallies' Sort of Pimento Cheese Sandwiches (pg. 40), and Chicken Salad in Pastry (pg. 37)

The Sandwiches

Here is what you need to know about picnic sandwiches—take these four recipes and don't look back. These are classics, the ones everybody requests, and the sandwiches I rely on for everything from picnics and cocktail parties, to a recent puppy-naming event. My son is such a fan of **Sallie's Sort of Pimento Cheese** that he once ate it at every meal for a week. That meant with everything from sandwiches to burgers, omelets, and even grits and nachos. It seemed crazy to me, but when he ran out he asked for more.

Classic Chicken Salad

INGREDIENTS

4 cups cooked chicken breast, chopped

½ cup celery, chopped (about 3 stalks)

2 hard-boiled eggs, chopped*

½ tsp celery seed

½ tsp pepper

1 Tbsp lemon juice

½ tsp salt (more to taste)

1¼ cups mayonnaise

Optional: 1 Tbsp parsley or tarragon chopped is very pretty and adds flavor

DIRECTIONS

Combine all ingredients in a large bowl.

Cover and chill until ready to use.

Keeps in the refrigerator for 3 days. (*hint: Excellent with any bread, in rolls, in phyllo cups, or stuffed in a tomato.*)

Makes 8 sandwiches.

Serving Suggestion: Make it Shrimp Salad by substituting shrimp for the chicken and adding a pinch of dill.

Egg Salad Sandwiches

These are a little different, but just perfect. Don't mash the yolks, it's a deal breaker.

INGREDIENTS

6 or 7 hard-boiled eggs, cooled and peeled*

1 stalk celery, minced

3 Tbsp green onion, chopped (about 2)

1 Tbsp sweet pickle, chopped, plus 1 tsp pickle juice

2 tsp fresh dill, chopped (or ¼ tsp dried)

¼ cup mayonnaise

½ tsp salt

½ tsp pepper

Optional: 2 tsp chopped parsley

Optional: 1 Tbsp capers

To serve: Any bread is fine. I like whole wheat with egg sandwiches.

DIRECTIONS

Chop eggs. (Cut in half, then fourths and chop into small bits, just don't mash them.)

Add chopped eggs to a mixing bowl and add celery, green onion, pickles and juice, dill, parsley, and capers.

Gently stir in mayonnaise, salt, and pepper.

Taste for seasonings.

Makes 5 sandwiches

*How to hard-boil an egg: Put the eggs in a pot of cold water and bring to a boil. Once the water is fully boiling, cover the pot, remove from heat, and let stand 12 to 14 minutes. Crack eggs (I shake them in the pan to crack). Replace water in the pan with ice and cold water to cool eggs. Let eggs cool thoroughly before peeling.

Sallie's Sort of Pimento Cheese

INGREDIENTS

1½ cups freshly grated sharp cheddar cheese

1½ cups freshly grated Monterey Jack pepper cheese (sub regular for hot pepper to get a milder taste)

1 cup mayonnaise

1 clove garlic, finely minced

¼ cup chopped olives (or just pimentos if you're being traditional)

1 tsp salt

2 Tbsp sherry

DIRECTIONS

Mix everything together and taste for seasonings.

Makes about 4 cups

Serving Suggestion: This is not just for sandwiches! Serve with celery and peppers or crackers, top a grilled burger, or stir it into cooked macaroni for a jazzy mac and cheese. The sky's the limit!

BONUS RECIPE:
Rosé Spritzers (my favorite picnic drink)

In a large pitcher or container, combine 1 cup sliced strawberries with 1 cup cubed watermelon. Pour in 2 bottles of chilled rosé and 1 bottle of chilled sparkling wine. Mint optional.

Cream Cheese, Olive, and Pecan Sandwiches

My mom made these all the time when I was little. It always seemed so elegant.

INGREDIENTS

1 (8-oz) package cream cheese, softened

½ cup pimento stuffed olives, drained and chopped

1 cup chopped pecans, toasted (can do carefully in the microwave)

2 Tbsp mayonnaise, enough to create spreading consistency

DIRECTIONS

Combine all ingredients.

(hint: We like to spread this on flour tortillas, roll them up, and slice them about an inch thick. We proudly call it Southern Sushi.)

Makes 6 whole sandwiches

Don't forget **Country Ham Salad Sandwiches** *(pg. 21)*

Make It a Picnic

Mix and match sandwich-filling choices. Use any bread you like—rolls, even tortillas. Consider packing containers of the sandwich ingredients and bread, and let everyone make their own sandwiches. If children are involved, don't forget the peanut butter. Pair with a cold soup from the *Chilled Soups to Go (pg. 30)* section and a dessert like **Ice Cream Muffins** *(pg. 57)*. You can't go wrong by including a bag of potato chips. Iced tea, wine, beer, water, and soft drinks that are chilled help to keep everything cold along with freezable ice packs.

V
Five Festive Brunches

Hosting a brunch is one of the best ways to entertain. Just the word implies lazy, leisurely late mornings that last until the afternoon, with good friends and good food. A brunch can be based around a well-thought-out and pre-planned menu, like the **Honey Bourbon Glazed Ham with Buttermilk Biscuits** *(pg. 52)*, or be as simple as putting together the ingredients for **Company Breakfast Strata** *(pg. 48)*, which takes less than 15 minutes, and calling a few friends to come enjoy it with you. Remember to brew some coffee!

If you do plan on a fancy brunch, there are several tips to help you have a good time at your own party. Here is a good one: set the table the night before and put out ingredients that don't need refrigeration. Also, mix ingredients or have them on hand for drinks. Don't include only recipes that require last minute preparations. For example, you can make **Baked French Toast** *(pg. 44)* and **Simple Homemade Sausage** *(pg. 46)* the day before, or early in the morning, and put the casserole in the oven to bake while you get to visit with guests. Reheat the sausage in the oven, or microwave during the last few minutes the casserole is baking. Or impress everyone with your skills and cook it for your audience. Lots of people will be willing to taste! Another great tip is to ask one of your friends to help with drinks and coffee duty. Nobody minds pitching in. A party favor is a charming idea—try serving mimosas in inexpensive champagne glasses purchased from a discount store or ordered online. Print guests' names on the glasses with permanent glass markers and invite your guests to take them home!

Two last tips—planning as much as you can ahead of time gives you the opportunity to enjoy your party, so make sure you do! And the last tip: never ever make omelets for a group of more than four people. I speak from an experience that will not be shared. It did involve throwing away a pan, plus a bagel run. But the mimosas and **Bonus Recipe: Honey Bourbon Bacon** *(pg. 84)* were fantastic, and a good playlist kept the party humming along.

Baked French Toast and Simple Homemade Sausage

This recipe brings great memories. When I was a high school counselor and sponsored student council, the officers met with me every Thursday during lunchtime. It was nice of them to give up their free time, and they always looked hungry, so I got in the habit of making lunch for them. That was a double crockpot investment, but besides many slow cooker chilies and soups, we frequently made use of an old oven and feasted on this **Baked French Toast**. It was their favorite and most requested treat. I like to serve it with **Simple Homemade Sausage** *(pg.46)*.

INGREDIENTS

1 loaf French bread (13 to 16 oz), cubed

8 eggs

3 cups half & half (or 2 cups milk and 1 cup cream)

¼ cup sugar

½ cup brown sugar

1 Tbsp vanilla

1 tsp cinnamon

½ tsp nutmeg

½ tsp salt

Brown Sugar Topping

½ cup flour

¾ cup brown sugar

1 tsp cinnamon

¼ tsp nutmeg

¼ tsp salt

1 stick butter (½ cup)

Optional: ½ cup finely chopped pecans

DIRECTIONS

Spray a 9 x 13 or similar size baking dish with cooking spray.

Preheat the oven to 350 degrees if you plan to bake this immediately.

(hint: The French Toast can be covered, refrigerated, and baked the next day.)

Break eggs into a large bowl and whisk to combine.

Add half & half (or milk mixture), sugar, brown sugar, vanilla, cinnamon, nutmeg, and salt, and whisk to thoroughly incorporate all ingredients.

Place cubed bread in the prepared baking dish and pour the egg mixture over it, stirring and making sure as much egg mixture is absorbed as possible.

To make topping, combine all ingredients in a bowl or in a food processor and mix until they resemble small crumbs.

If you are baking the French Toast immediately, sprinkle topping evenly over the bread mixture.

If you plan to bake it the next day, store the topping covered in a bowl or in a baggie, to top the French Toast right before baking.

Bake the French Toast for 45 to 55 minutes until the top is crispy and the center is set.

Serve with butter and maple syrup.

Serves 8 to 10

Simple Homemade Sausage

It's so easy and so delicious you'll never buy prepackaged again. Best of all, you control the ingredients—always a plus!

INGREDIENTS

1 lb ground pork	4 cloves garlic, very finely chopped
1 lb ground turkey (can use all pork or all turkey)	2 tsp salt
¼ cup maple syrup (the real stuff)	¼ tsp red pepper flakes (more to taste)
1 Tbsp fresh thyme, chopped (½ tsp dried)	½ tsp black pepper
1½ Tbsp fresh sage, chopped (so much better fresh, but ½ tsp dried is ok)	Canola oil for cooking

DIRECTIONS

Thoroughly mix all ingredients except canola oil.

Shape into approximately 20 patties about ⅓-inch thick. *(hint: Sausage patties can be refrigerated or frozen until ready to use.)*

To cook, heat a skillet coated with canola oil over medium high heat.

Add sausage patties and cook on each side until nicely browned.

Drain on paper towels.

Serves 10

Serving Suggestion: The sausage is wonderful with **Buttermilk Biscuits** *(pg. 54).*

Make It a Brunch

Assembling the **French Toast** and making sausage patties a day ahead will make this brunch a breeze. Add a fruit salad with berries and pre-cut melon from the grocery store salad bar. Make a dressing of ½ cup sour cream, 1 Tbsp honey, and 1 tsp poppy seeds. A mimosa is perfect for almost any brunch—particularly this one. It's just orange juice and sparkling wine or champagne, so let guests make their own while you show off by cooking the **Simple Homemade Sausage**. If that's too much trouble, cook it ahead and reheat in the microwave. Serve this brunch buffet style, and make a big pot of coffee with mugs, cream, and sugar available.

Chilaquiles with Eggs

One of my son's college friends is from San Antonio. When my son first visited it took him about 15 seconds to fall in love with both San Antonio and *chilaquiles*. It took us several tries to get this outstanding recipe. It took me longer to learn to say it right. But falling in love with *chilaquiles* was no problem at all.

INGREDIENTS

2 Tbsp canola oil

10 medium corn tortillas, cut (or torn) into about 6 pieces each

16 oz salsa (**Bonus Recipe: Roasted Tomato Salsa** *(pg. 56)*, or buy your favorite)

6 eggs

To serve: crumbled cojita or queso fresco cheese (sub feta if you can't find either)

DIRECTIONS

Preheat the oven to 350 degrees.

Line a baking sheet with aluminum foil.

Spread tortilla pieces on baking sheet and bake 10 to 12 minutes, until the edges start to brown and they are crisp.

Remove tortillas from the oven, and preheat oven to broil.

Heat oil in a large iron or ovenproof skillet over medium high heat.

Add tortillas and salsa, reduce heat, and allow the tortillas and salsa to simmer for about 5 minutes.

Gently crack eggs on top of salsa and broil under preheated broiler until yolks are set and centers are still a bit runny, 3 to 4 minutes.

Crumble cheese over the top.

Serves 6

Make It a Brunch

This makes for a totally entertaining presentation, if you deliver the dish right to the table and serve out of the skillet. It's informal, and guests will love it. Also, it is very easy to double the recipe using a second skillet. Serve with **Bonus Recipe: Honey Bourbon Bacon** *(pg. 84)* that can be prepared ahead of time. Make a special treat with the **Bonus Recipe: Party Watermelon** *(pg. 85)*. Then you have your fruit salad, your cocktail, and dessert all rolled up in one neat little dish.

Company Breakfast Strata

This is not your mother's Christmas morning casserole. The addition of red and green roasted peppers, the combination of cheeses, and the nice thick French bread make this a brand-new treat. Plus, you can assemble it the day before—perfect for entertaining.

INGREDIENTS

1 loaf thick French bread (13 to 16 oz), cut in ½ inch slices

⅓ cup canned diced green chilies*

⅓ cup sliced roasted red peppers from a jar*

6 green onions, sliced

1 lb breakfast sausage, cooked and crumbled (*hint: You can cook ahead and freeze; also, you can easily substitute diced ham or make without meat for a vegetarian dish, or use* **Simple Homemade Sausage** *(pg. 46).)*

1½ cups sharp cheddar cheese, grated

1½ cups Monterey Jack cheese, grated

12 eggs

4 cups half & half or whole milk

1½ tsp salt

1 tsp black pepper

*You can sauté one half each red and green pepper if desired, to replace the canned green chilies and jarred red peppers.

DIRECTIONS

Spray a 9 x 13 or equivalent size casserole with cooking spray.

In a large bowl, whisk eggs, half & half, salt, and pepper until thoroughly combined.

Cover the bottom of the casserole with half of the sliced bread.

Top bread slices with half of the sausage, half of the red and green peppers, half of the onions, and half of each cheese.

Pour half of the custard mixture over the first layer.

Make a second layer of bread, remaining sausage, peppers, onions, and cheese.

Pour remaining custard mixture over the top.

Allow the casserole to sit for at least 20 minutes before baking. (You can assemble and refrigerate the casserole up to 2 days before baking.)

Preheat the oven to 325 degrees.

Bake for about 50 minutes (1 hour if made ahead) until custard is just set.

If desired, broil for a couple of minutes to brown the top.

Try really hard to wait five minutes before cutting and serving.

The recipe can be halved or doubled depending on your crowd.

Serves 12

Make It a Brunch

This dish has everything, but **Bonus Recipe: Citrus and Avocado Salad** *(pg. 56)*, would be a pretty addition. You can serve fruit tea and everyone will love it, or maybe offer a brunch cocktail? **Grapefruit Margaritas** are easy. Keep it light with one cup of tequila to 6 cups grapefruit juice and a thin slice of fresh jalapeño for a spicy touch. Make a batch of **My Honey's Muffins** *(pg.*97) and put them on the table in a basket lined with a colorful napkin. They are great with the salad and will satisfy any sweet tooth.

Ham, Onion, and Gruyère Quiche

This is a perfect brunch, lunch, or dinner entrée. Cold leftovers are also delicious cut in little bites and served as hors d'oeuvres. The good news is the onions cook in the oven, so you don't have to spend a lot of time stirring and sautéing. The sugar helps them caramelize. This will be a family favorite.

INGREDIENTS

½ stick butter (4 Tbsp)

3 onions, diced (sweet onions like Vidalia are a good choice)

1 tsp salt

2 tsp sugar

¼ lb ham, diced (*hint: Ask the deli for a ¼ lb piece of ham unsliced so you can cut it in small, bite-size pieces.*)

½ cup sherry

4 eggs

1¼ cups heavy cream

½ tsp nutmeg

1 tsp black pepper

½ tsp salt

1 cup grated gruyère cheese

1 unbaked pie shell, purchased or **Pie Crust** recipe *(pg. 165)* (can also be baked in individual pie shells)*

DIRECTIONS

Preheat the oven to 350 degrees.

Melt 3 Tbsp butter in a large Dutch oven or pot with a lid.

Add onions, 1 tsp salt, and 2 tsp sugar, and stir until onions are thoroughly coated with butter.

Cover the pot with a lid and place in the oven for an hour.

Melt 1 Tbsp butter in a large skillet over high heat.

Add ham and sherry and cook, stirring for 2 minutes.

Remove pan from heat.

In a large bowl, whisk together eggs, cream, nutmeg, pepper, and salt.

Add ham, cheese, and onions, and stir to combine.

Pour into pie shell and bake for 45 to 50 minutes until set.

Cool slightly before cutting.

Can be served hot or at room temperature.

Serves 6 to 8

*Quiche mixture can be baked in mini-muffin tins without crusts and sprayed with cooking spray for small crust-less quiches.

Make It a Brunch

Since this can be served warm or at room temperature, it's a very easy dish for hosting company. A tossed salad is a fine addition, but **The Accidental Salad** *(pg. 64)* is very pretty with lots of vegetables, and so easy to make ahead of time. You don't have to serve bread with quiche, but the **Bonus Recipe: Ice Cream Muffins** *(pg. 57)* has two ingredients and can be made in any flavor—I think strawberry would be nice. Your guests will love them.

Honey Bourbon Glazed Ham and Buttermilk Biscuits

Yes, you can absolutely track down a store specializing in ham and spend a fortune for a less than spectacular one. But why do that when, with very little effort, you can prepare a remarkable ham, flavored with honey and bourbon, right in your own kitchen at about one-tenth of the price? It is quite an impressive presentation. Your guests will be amazed. We are from the South, so we've always loved our bourbon, but we have just become beekeepers and now proudly cook with lots of honey. Become a fan of local honey—it's marvelous.

INGREDIENTS

One 12- to 15-lb bone-in cooked ham

1½ cups bourbon

1 cup honey

½ tsp red pepper flakes

½ tsp black pepper

DIRECTIONS

Preheat the oven to 350 degrees.

Whisk bourbon, honey, red pepper flakes, and black pepper together in a medium bowl.

Set ham on a rack in a large roasting pan and pour in 2 cups water. (*hint: You don't have to buy a roasting pan; a 9 x 13 roasting rack is much cheaper and you will find lots of uses for it—like cooling cakes and cookies. You can also find roasting pans made of disposable aluminum at most grocery stores.*)

Score ham in a crosshatch pattern, barely cutting through both lengthwise and across to make 1-inch square patterns.

Brush ham with bourbon mixture every 20 minutes.

Roast for 1½ to 2 hours or until a meat thermometer reads 135 degrees.

Transfer ham to a cutting board and let rest 15 minutes before slicing. (*hint: It is delicious cold in sandwiches over the next few days.*)

Buttermilk Biscuits

INGREDIENTS

2 cups self-rising flour* (*hint: You can prepare biscuits ahead of time and store the unbaked biscuits in the fridge for a few hours until the ham is ready.*)

1 tsp sugar

½ stick cold butter (4 Tbsp), cut in small pieces

¾ cup buttermilk**

DIRECTIONS

Preheat the oven to 425 degrees.

Line a baking sheet with parchment paper, or lightly spray with cooking spray.

In a large mixing bowl or a food processor, combine flour, sugar and butter. (*hint: Mixing by hand will yield flakier biscuits.*)

Add buttermilk until just blended.

On a floured work area, roll or pat out dough about an inch thick and cut with a biscuit cutter or small glass dipped in flour. (*hint: Using waxed paper for the floured surface area makes for an easy cleanup.*)

Place biscuits on prepared baking sheet.

Re-roll and cut scraps into more biscuits.

Bake for 12 to 15 minutes until lightly browned.

Brush with melted butter for a pretty biscuit!

*To make **self-rising flour**, mix 2 cups flour with 1 Tbsp baking powder and 1 tsp salt.

**If you don't have buttermilk, mix a Tbsp of vinegar or lemon juice in a cup of milk, let it sit a minute, and use in recipe.

Leftover Suggestion: See the recipe for **White Bean Soup** (*pg. 82*), or make a few ham sandwiches. Check the picnic chapter for more recipes for a fun picnic.

Make It a Brunch

Truly there is nothing more impressive than pulling your own ham right out of the oven. Let the ham rest while you put the biscuits you made ahead of time in to bake. Talk about a showstopper! It's brunch, and that is a great excuse for making **Bonus Recipe: Cheese Grits** (*pg. 57*). Add a tasty fruit salad (grocery store salad bar), or let this party be a potluck with your gorgeous ham as the centerpiece. Invite guests to bring a favorite side dish or ingredients for a **Bloody Mary** (*pg. 15*). Put out butter, honey, jam, mustard—anything that goes well with ham and biscuits.

Company Breakfast Strata (pg. 48)

CITRUS AND AVOCADO SALAD

Peel, section, and seed 2 grapefruits and 2 oranges. Peel 2 avocados, remove pits, and cube. Thinly slice ¼ red onion. Layer a salad bowl with red or green lettuce, and top with grapefruit, oranges, avocado, and red onion. Sprinkle with sunflower seeds if desired. Chopped olives are also a nice touch. Dressing: In a jar, combine 2 Tbsp white wine vinegar with 2 Tbsp orange juice, ¼ cup olive oil, ½ tsp salt, ½ tsp pepper and 1 Tbsp sugar. Shake it up and pour over the salad.

ROASTED TOMATO SALSA

Preheat broiler, line a rimmed baking pan with aluminum foil, and spray with cooking spray. Drain a 28-oz can of whole tomatoes (reserve juice) and place tomatoes in the baking pan along with 4 halved and seeded jalapeños, 4 peeled garlic cloves, 1 red pepper seeded and quartered, and one small onion, peeled and quartered (optional: 1 seeded, dried pasalli chili). Pour 1 Tbsp olive oil over the top and broil for 15 to 20 minutes to slightly brown vegetables. Cool enough to add to a food processor or blender. Add juice of one lime, 2 Tbsp cilantro leaves, and 1 tsp salt. Pulse a few times for a chunky consistency. Add reserved tomato liquid if needed for thinning salsa.

ICE CREAM MUFFINS

Preheat oven to 425 degrees. Spray a muffin pan with cooking spray. In a mixing bowl, combine 1 pint of mostly melted ice cream with 2 cups self-rising flour (see pg. 54 to make your own). Full-fat ice cream is necessary, or the consistency won't be right. Fill muffin cups three-fourths of the way up and bake for 10 to 12 minutes. Sprinkle tops with sugar if desired. My friend's original recipe called for vanilla ice cream from Nashville's own Candyland, but other flavors are great as well—like strawberry. Yum.

CHEESE GRITS

In a large saucepan bring 2 cups water and 2 cups whole milk to a boil. Stir in 1 clove minced garlic and 1½ tsp salt. Slowly whisk in 1 cup dry grits. Reduce heat to moderately low, and cook, stirring frequently until grits are tender, about 20 minutes. Remove saucepan from heat, and stir in 4 oz sharp cheddar cheese (you can experiment with cheese—but cheddar is a pretty classic touch), ½ tsp pepper, and 4 Tbsp butter. Serve hot!

VI
Six Simple Salads

Sometimes a salad is the best part of a meal. It can be light and refreshing, or even a main course. Throughout this cookbook, you'll find several salad recipes listed as **Bonus Recipes** that are presented to accompany a meal. Mix and match those salads as well as these six favorites, and enjoy the different flavors and ingredients. Add vegetables and fruits that you like. Experiment with dressings using flavored vinegars, citrus juice, and different oils. Choose herbs that taste good to you and—as I always say—use what you have on hand. Before you know it, you'll be creating your own masterpiece salads.

These six salads are some of our favorites and are versatile enough to make most of the year with produce available, and delicious enough to please the pickiest palate. Some of these salads, like the **Peas and Crumbled Bacon Salad** *(pg. 61)* and the **Tomatoes, Potatoes, and Green Bean Salad** *(pg. 66),* are excellent additions to a picnic or potluck, and just as delicious a day after they are prepared. **The Accidental Salad** *(pg. 64)* can be put together with ingredients from your pantry and freezer—no grocery run involved. The **Tomato and Grilled Bread Salad** *(pg. 65)* can easily serve as a main course using grilled meat, poultry, or fish.

Remember that when you entertain, you do not want to be running around trying to create and serve last minute dishes. All of the salads you find here are easy to prepare ahead of time, or they only require a quick toss in homemade dressing with ingredients you've put in a jar, ready to shake up and pour. A salad doesn't have to be served as a first course (that can be a lot of work), but a wonderful salad can elevate any meal to new heights. These are salad recipes your family and your guests will love, and you will too, not only because they taste so good, but also because you know how easy they are to prepare.

Apples and Brussels Sprouts Salad

This salad will convert any Brussels sprouts hater, especially if you don't tell them what it is. In my house, that's not sneaky, it's just self-preservation. This is a beautiful fall salad, but delicious any time of year.

INGREDIENTS

½ lb Brussels sprouts, thinly sliced (I use the slicer on my food processor, but slicing is easy to do by hand)

1 small apple, cored and thinly sliced

1 Tbsp fresh tarragon leaves, thinly sliced (or ½ tsp dried)

½ onion, thinly sliced

½ cup toasted walnuts (you could use any nuts you like or have on hand)

¼ cup blue cheese, crumbled

Salt and pepper to taste

Maple Mustard Dressing

2 Tbsp sherry or balsamic vinegar

2 Tbsp maple syrup (real)

2 Tbsp olive oil

1 tsp honey or Dijon mustard

1 clove garlic, minced

DIRECTIONS

Combine salad ingredients in a large bowl.

Combine dressing ingredients in a jar and shake it up.

Pour dressing over salad and serve.

Serves 4 to 6

Peas and Crumbled Bacon Salad

There is broccoli salad, and then there is seven-layer salad, which can now take a back seat and make way for the perfect combination of both—**Peas and Crumbled Bacon Salad**. The mix of crunchy bacon and cheese with the sweet snap of green peas is nothing short of divine. Best news: if you are lucky and have leftovers, it's honestly better the next day. Should we name it "Peas in Paradise"?

INGREDIENTS

1 (16-oz) package frozen peas, thawed

8 to 10 slices bacon, cooked and crumbled

⅓ cup mayonnaise

⅓ cup sharp cheddar cheese, grated

¼ onion, finely chopped

½ tsp salt

½ tsp pepper

½ tsp sugar

2 Tbsp sunflower seeds

Optional: for serving, lettuce and sliced cherry tomatoes

DIRECTIONS

Mix peas, bacon, mayonnaise, cheese, and onion together.

Stir in salt, pepper, and sugar, and taste for seasonings.

Top with sunflower seeds.

Serves 8 to 10

Serving Suggestion: Line a plate with lettuce, and mound **Peas and Crumbled Bacon Salad** on top. Garnish with sunflower seeds. If desired, place a few sliced cherry tomatoes around the edges of the plate.

Summer Succotash Salad

Succotash is an amazing comfort food that has sort of gone out of style, but not in our house. We like it so much that I had to create a summer version.

INGREDIENTS

½ lb fresh okra, 25 to 30 pods

2 cups butterbeans or lady peas, cooked (can use frozen if fresh aren't available)

2 ears of corn, kernels cut from corn (hint: *If corn is very fresh, it doesn't have to be cooked.*)

2 cups cherry tomatoes, sliced

½ red onion, sliced

1 bunch arugula or other lettuce

2 Tbsp olive oil

1 Tbsp blackening or Cajun seasoning

Optional garnish: Parmesan cheese shavings (use vegetable peeler)

Dressing

6 Tbsp balsamic or lemon balsamic vinegar

4 Tbsp olive oil

1 clove garlic, finely minced

2 tsp sugar

1 tsp salt

1 tsp pepper

Combine dressing ingredients in a jar and shake it up

DIRECTIONS

Line a serving plate with arugula or lettuce.

Mix together butterbeans, corn, cherry tomatoes, and onion, and put mixture on top of arugula.

In a small skillet, bring about one inch of water to a boil. *(hint: Use same skillet to blacken okra for easy cleanup.)*

Add okra and boil for one minute.

Remove okra, rinse under cold water, and cut each pod in half length-wise.

Wipe skillet dry and return it to the stove.

Heat olive oil in the skillet over high heat and add okra.

Add the seasoning and toss okra to coat.

Cook until slightly browned, 2 to 3 minutes.

Top salad with okra, pour dressing over the top, and add Parmesan cheese if desired.

Serves 8 to 10

Serving Suggestion: Marvelous with anything grilled; in fact, you could blacken the okra on the grill, too, after par boiling and coating with oil and spice. Add grilled chicken to the salad, and it's a summer feast. If your grill stays warm, make **Grilled Peaches with Ice Cream** *(pg. 160)* for dessert. That's a grilling party!

Preheat oven to 375 degrees. Line a baking sheet with parchment paper or spray with cooking spray. Drain 2 cans of chickpeas and spread on a clean dishtowel to dry for about 10 minutes. Put chickpeas on prepared pan, pour over about 2 Tbsp olive oil, and sprinkle with 1 to 2 tsp salt. You can also add hot paprika or cayenne to make them a bit spicier. Roll chickpeas around in oil and seasoning to coat, and roast for about 20 minutes. Remove pan and give chickpeas a stir. Return to the oven and bake another 30 minutes. Cool a few minutes before eating—they get crunchier as they cool.

The Accidental Salad

The story is almost as good as the salad. My study group was meeting for dinner at a friend's house. There were 25 guests, and the four of us who were hosting all had an assignment. I brought a pasta casserole, someone else brought dessert, and another wine. Somehow the hostess, whose home we were meeting in, missed the part where she provided a salad. She is a lovely, charming person, but not a cook. Her fridge contained an apple and some interesting condiments, but thankfully her freezer was a treasure trove, and her pantry had lots of great stuff that had never been touched. Here is what I made. We still laugh about it, but now I make it all the time—to rave reviews.

INGREDIENTS

2 (12-oz) packages frozen green beans

1 (10- to 12-oz) package frozen asparagus

1 package frozen, shelled edamame

1 cup toasted almonds (Toast them in the microwave on a paper towel, checking after one minute. They usually take about 2 minutes to lightly toast.)

1 cup dried cranberries (or whatever is on hand: raisins, cherries etc.)

Salt and pepper to taste

DIRECTIONS

Put vegetables in a large microwave-safe bowl, and microwave until no longer frozen but not yet heated through. (Stir every minute to check, about 4 minutes.)

Drain any liquid from cooking and add almonds, cranberries, and bottled Asian-style dressing or **Bonus Recipe: Sesame Dressing**, and mix thoroughly.

Add salt and pepper to taste.

Serves 10

In a jar with a lid, combine ½ cup rice vinegar, 2 Tbsp mirin (Japanese sweet cooking wine, found in the Asian section of the grocery), 2 Tbsp canola oil, 2 tsp sesame oil, 3 Tbsp sugar, 2 Tbsp soy sauce, ¼ tsp salt, 1 Tbsp sesame seeds. Shake it up in the jar. Makes about ¾ cup

Tomato and Grilled Bread Salad

My husband is not a connoisseur of fresh produce—a nice way of saying he hates vegetables. But he adores this salad, and he'll request it even in the dead of winter when tomatoes are at their lowest point. We've been making **Tomato and Grilled Bread Salad** the same way for years. All that varies is the cheese, depending on what we have in the fridge, and the tomatoes, which depend on the season and the garden.

INGREDIENTS

5 or 6 ripe tomatoes cut in bite-size pieces *(hint: Obviously vine-ripened summer tomatoes are best, but if you crave this salad in the middle of the winter, seek out vine-ripened tomatoes, or use romas, adding in a few more if they are small.)*

1 clove garlic, minced

½ onion, diced

6 to 8 fresh basil leaves, torn into pieces

3 Tbsp olive oil

2 Tbsp balsamic vinegar

1 tsp salt

1 tsp sugar

⅛ tsp red pepper flakes

Parmesan or other favorite cheese, grated or crumbled

To serve: French or Italian bread, olive oil, and salt

DIRECTIONS

Combine all ingredients but the bread.

Allow mixture to sit at room temperature at least 30 minutes or up to 6 hours.

Brush both sides of the bread lightly with olive oil, and sprinkle with a pinch of salt.

If you are grilling, toast bread on the grill until it is browned with grill marks.

If you aren't using a grill, place bread on a baking sheet and put under a preheated broiler, turning once to brown each side.

Cut or tear bread in bite-size pieces, and mix with salad ingredients.

Top with cheese.

Serves 4

Serving Suggestion: This is wonderful with grilled steak, chicken, or fish. It's perfect for a party, because you can make the salad well ahead of time and grill everything else later. Add corn to the grill, or serve with baked potatoes for the easiest cleanup ever.

Tomatoes, Potatoes, and Green Bean Salad

I was cooking for a summery picnic, and a guest requested potato salad. I love cold mayonnaise-coated potatoes as much as the next girl—really, I do—but produce was pretty, and I was craving something different. This was exactly it. This salad is good with anything, cold or at room temp. No worries of warm mayo, and best of all, everyone loves it.

INGREDIENTS

2 lb baby potatoes (really pretty if you can find different colors)

1 Tbsp salt

½ lb green beans, cut in bite-size pieces

1 pint cherry or grape tomatoes, halved (mix of colors great here as well)

1 small red onion, thinly sliced

2 to 3 Tbsp capers, drained (can substitute finely chopped green olives)

¼ cup olive oil

¼ cup balsamic vinegar

1 tsp sugar

½ cup chopped parsley (Sometimes I use tarragon because it's my favorite fresh herb.)

1 tsp pepper

½ tsp salt (more to taste)

DIRECTIONS

Cover potatoes with cold water in a large saucepan and bring to a boil.

Add 1 Tbsp salt, reduce heat, and simmer for 10 to 15 minutes or until potatoes are tender.

Remove potatoes with a slotted spoon, and add green beans to the same pot.

Cook green beans until barely tender, about 3 minutes.

Drain green beans and cover with cold water.

Drain again when cool.

Cut potatoes in half and add to a large serving bowl.

Add green beans, tomatoes, onion, and capers.

Pour olive oil, vinegar, and sugar in a clean jar with a lid and shake well to combine.

Pour dressing over vegetables.

Add parsley, pepper, and salt, and stir to thoroughly coat with dressing.

Serves 8 to 10

Serving Suggestion: Excellent with any grilled meat, including chicken or fish. This is also a wonderful addition to a potluck party. Top with **Bonus Recipe: Crispy Chickpeas** *(pg.63)* for a crunchy bite. Or pass them with the salad for a fun, crispy snack.

VII
Seven Soups for Supper

Can a soup supper be a dinner party? Absolutely. Everyone loves soup. When I was younger and living with several girls in a rental house, we regularly had "Sunday Soup Night" and invited friends, and boyfriends if we had them, to come have soup and bread. Dessert was potluck—ice cream was a favorite. We thought it was very sophisticated, and we always talked about what we were reading. Potentially, we were a book club before its time.

I still love to serve soup as a main course at a party. Add a salad and some bread and everyone is charmed by your simple but lovely dinner. I learned a lesson about soup when my husband and I moved into our current home. I organized a dinner party to get to know a few new neighbors. The guests were invited, the menu planned, and the table set before my husband informed me that he could not have any meat, fish, or poultry for the next two days due to an upcoming routine medical exam. I was still enough of a newlywed to not strangle him on site (my first instinct), but to instead change the menu, which had been based around a seafood pasta designed to impress. We had **Roasted Tomato Soup** *(pg. 76)* with cheese toasts, and a **Bonus Recipe: Spinach and Artichoke Heart Salad** *(pg. 11)*. It's possible I got more compliments for that dinner than ever before. I should invite the same group back and serve **Steak, Stout, and Spuds Soup** *(pg. 80)* just to prove that I know how to cook with a good piece of ribeye steak and still serve soup.

My mother always said, dinners don't have to be fancy to impress; if you serve food that tastes good, everyone will be delighted. However, she did give me six elegant antique soupspoons.

Chicken and Dumplings with Herbs

The saying "everything old is new again" was never more true than in the world of food. My sister recently went to an upscale dinner cooked by a well-known celebrity chef, and Chicken and Dumplings was on the menu. I'm not surprised. My guys ask for it all the time. It's comfort food, but it's also a classic. Plus, here is a secret you don't have to share: dumplings are ridiculously easy to make! This is not exactly a soup, but a bowl and spoon are necessary, so it definitely makes the cut.

INGREDIENTS

3 cups cooked chicken, cubed (I like to cook 2 large chicken breasts in the broth with a carrot and celery, but rotisserie is fine too.)

6 cups chicken broth

2 cups flour (extra for rolling)

1 tsp baking powder

½ tsp salt

1 tsp black pepper

2 Tbsp fresh herbs (any combination of thyme, parsley, sage, or chives), or 1 Tbsp dried

3 Tbsp butter

1 cup milk

Optional: frozen peas

DIRECTIONS

In a large Dutch oven or pot, bring broth to a simmer.

In a food processor, with an electric mixer, or by hand, combine flour, baking powder, salt, pepper, and herbs (pre-chop herbs if using a mixer or mixing by hand), and give it a few spins to chop herbs.

Add butter and process (or mix) to incorporate.

Add milk and blend until a soft dough forms.

On a floured surface, roll the dough to about ¼ inch thickness (or thinner for thinner dumplings).

Cut into strips about an inch in diameter—perfection won't win any prizes here; scruffy pieces taste just as good.

Toss with a little more flour so they won't stick, and drop into simmering broth.

Cook for about 20 minutes, stirring occasionally.

Add chicken, and peas if desired, to heat through.

Serve, enjoy, and hope for leftovers!

Serves 6 to 8, easy to double

Make It a Soup Supper

Honestly, **Chicken and Dumplings** is an occasion all by itself, but if you want to be a bit fancy, the **Apples and Brussels Sprouts Salad** *(pg.60)* is a beautiful contrast, with the crunchy apples and tangy dressing. A microbrew would be a fun choice to serve with this dinner, but open a chardonnay for your wine drinkers. Pass an easy dessert like **Blondies with Dark Roots** *(pg.164)* for a perfect ending.

Classic Beer and Cheese Soup

My family and friends have fallen in love with this soup. It's hard to not like a soup made with cheese and beer. One thing I enjoy about this particular recipe is that I get to include my guys' hobby of brewing beer, and peppers from my son's hot pepper garden. I like to think it's a group participation recipe. However, if you don't make your own beer or grow your own peppers, it's ok. The grocery store has your back.

INGREDIENTS

½ stick butter (4 Tbsp)

1 onion, chopped (*hint: If you have a food processor, you can chop all of these vegetables together with a couple of quick pulses.*)

1 carrot, peeled and chopped

2 ribs of celery, chopped

3 cloves garlic, minced

½ jalapeño, chopped (seeds optional for more heat)

1 tsp fresh thyme (or ½ tsp dried)

¼ cup flour

4 cups chicken broth

12 oz dark beer

4 oz white cheddar, grated (If you can't find it, ask at the grocery store deli.)

12 oz sharp cheddar, grated

1 cup half & half

½ tsp Worcestershire sauce

DIRECTIONS

Melt butter in a large Dutch oven or pot over medium high heat.

When butter is melted, add onion, carrot, celery, garlic, jalapeño pepper, and thyme.

Lower heat to medium and sauté vegetables for 8 to 10 minutes until softened.

Add flour and stir for another minute.

Add chicken broth and stir to combine with flour mixture.

Stir in beer and Worcestershire sauce and allow soup to simmer for 20 minutes stirring occasionally.

Add in cheeses and cream and stir to melt cheese.

Optional: Top with **Bonus Recipe: Honey Bourbon Bacon**

Serves 4 to 6 for dinner, 8 as a first course

Make It a Soup Supper

We like to serve this with large pretzels (you can find them in the grocery freezer section) and mustard. Some recipes call for mustard in the soup, but we like it on the side. Top the soup with crumbled **Bonus Recipe: Honey Bourbon Bacon** *(pg. 84)* for an extra delicious touch. Make a big batch of **Oatmeal Raisin Cookies** *(pg. 168)* for dessert.

Honey Bourbon Bacon (pg. 84)

Italian Wedding Soup

This soup has nothing to do with an actual wedding, but is supposed to be a marriage between the meat and vegetables. Does that make the pasta a third wheel? We love it all, but the tiny meatballs do make **Italian Wedding Soup** extra special. Maybe someone will propose if you serve them this soup, even if you are already married—in which case the correct answer is, "No, but thank you!"

INGREDIENTS

Meatballs

1 lb ground meat (turkey, chicken, or beef)

¼ cup panko or bread crumbs

¼ cup Parmesan cheese, grated

1 egg

1 Tbsp olive oil

Splash of white wine (about 2 Tbsp)

1 tsp salt

1 tsp oregano

½ tsp pepper

2 cloves garlic, minced

Soup

1 onion, minced

2 carrots, sliced (about 1 cup)

2 stalks celery, sliced (about 1 cup)

Optional: cabbage, about 1 cup chopped

1 Tbsp olive oil

8 cups chicken or vegetable broth

½ cup white wine

½ tsp dried basil

1 (15-oz) can navy or cannellini beans, drained and rinsed

2 cups loosely-packed, leafy greens (Kale, escarole, and spinach are all good choices.)

1 cup of any small dried pasta

Grated Parmesan cheese for topping*

DIRECTIONS

Preheat the oven to 350 degrees.

Line a baking sheet with aluminum foil and spray with cooking spray.

Use your hands to gently combine all ingredients for the meatballs in a large bowl, and roll into small balls, about ½ inch each. (*hint: Get your hands slightly damp and it's easier to roll the meatballs.*)

Place meatballs on prepared baking sheet and bake for about 20 minutes or until lightly browned.

While meatballs bake, sauté onions, carrots, celery, olive oil, and cabbage, if using it, in a large pot or Dutch oven until soft, about 5 minutes.

Add broth, wine, basil, and beans. (You may add more broth or water if your soup is too thick.)

Cook pasta according to directions and add to the soup. (If you cook pasta in the soup, it absorbs a lot of the liquid and may get mushy.)

Add leafy greens to the soup.

Add meatballs and heat through.

Serve topped with cheese.

Serves 6 to 8

*When you grate cheese down to the rind, don't throw it away—freeze it. Keep a freezer bag of cheese rinds to add to soups for lots of extra flavor. It won't melt into the soup, so remove before serving.

Make It a Soup Supper

This soup is definitely a crowd pleaser. A loaf of good bread to dip in the soup is a nice touch, or make **Bonus Recipe: Perfect Garlic Cheese Bread** *(pg. 158)* for a real treat. If you are serving pre-dinner cocktails, the **Rebujito** *(pg. 159)* is perfect with salty olives as a delightful snack—green Castelvetrano and black Kalamatas are my favorites. After a hot soup, a cool dessert can be refreshing, so try **Frozen Lemonade Pie** *(pg. 174).*

Roasted Tomato Soup

This is so amazing and so delicious, and not like anything you could ever buy in a can or box from the store. Really, it's minimal effort for maximum flavor. And oh, the smell—so good you'll wish it could be bottled! Perfect soup for a cool fall evening, a cozy winter night by the fire (or light candles—work with what you have), or for a chilly spring supper.

INGREDIENTS

1 cup beef or vegetable broth, divided

1 Tbsp brown sugar

3 Tbsp balsamic vinegar

1 Tbsp soy sauce

1 onion, chopped

5 garlic cloves, peeled

2 (28-oz) cans whole tomatoes, drained

½ cup half & half

Optional: cracked black pepper

DIRECTIONS

Preheat the oven to 450 degrees.

Line a rimmed baking sheet with aluminum foil, and spray with cooking spray.

Combine ½ cup of broth, sugar, vinegar, and soy sauce in a small bowl.

Place onion, garlic, and tomatoes on prepared baking sheet and pour broth mixture over tomato mixture.

Bake for 50 minutes or until vegetables are lightly browned.

Place the tomato mixture in a blender.

Add remaining ½ cup broth and half & half, and process until smooth.

Add more broth to thin if necessary.

Garnish with cracked black pepper if desired.

Serves 6 to 8

Serving Suggestion: If you must, strain the soup, but I would never throw away those delightful little roasted bits of tomato!

Make It a Soup Supper

You don't need much help here. The most fabulous accompaniment is **Bonus Recipe: Grilled Brie and Cheddar Sandwiches,** perfect for dipping. Red wine would be excellent, but so would cold milk. This is almost a pajama-party-perfect menu! Don't forget to pass **Best Chocolate Chip Cookies** *(pg. 169)*

Line a baking sheet with aluminum foil, and preheat broiler. For each sandwich, put 2 slices of bread (white or whole wheat) on the baking sheet. Cover one piece of bread with thin slices of brie cheese, rind removed, and one piece of bread with thin slices of sharp cheddar. Broil until just melted. In a large skillet over medium high heat, melt 1 Tbsp butter per sandwich. Put two sandwich halves together and grill in butter until browned on each side. Cut each sandwich in half and serve with soup.

Rotisserie Chicken Pho

This is my son's favorite soup. Most Japanese restaurants will not pack pho to go—it's not a good traveler. But sometimes you need your favorite soup in the comfort of your own home. A rotisserie chicken makes it easy and adds extra flavor to the broth.

INGREDIENTS

1 rotisserie chicken

1-inch piece of ginger, sliced (can be bought in a tube at most groceries if you don't have fresh)

4 carrots, 1 cut in chunks, 3 peeled and sliced

1 garlic clove, smashed

1 cinnamon stick

1 star anise (found in spice section of grocery store)

5 or 6 green onions, white part sliced and green part reserved

12 cups chicken broth

4 cups water

2 packages ramen noodles (discard flavor packs—or save for another use)

1 cup baby spinach

Optional: 1 cardamom seed (or powdered cardamom ⅛ tsp)

Optional garnish: 4 hard-boiled eggs, peeled and sliced in half; hot chili paste (Asian food section of the grocery store); soy sauce

DIRECTIONS

Cut away breast and leg portions of the rotisserie chicken.

Use your fingers to shred the meat, and set shredded meat in the refrigerator until broth is finished.

Break chicken carcass with any meat remaining into several pieces and add to a large Dutch oven or pot.

Add chicken broth and water to the pot along with the ginger, 1 peeled carrot, garlic, cinnamon stick, star anise, tops of green onions, and cardamom, if using.

Bring to a boil, then lower to a simmer and cook until reduced by about one third, occasionally skimming the top to remove any grease, about one hour.

Strain broth completely and discard solids.*

Return broth to the pot, add 3 peeled and sliced carrots, and simmer for 10 minutes.

Cook noodles in salted water according to package directions.

Add shredded chicken, cooked noodles, and spinach leaves to the pot, and heat through.

Taste for salt (broth has different levels of salt)

Serve topped with sliced green onions, soy sauce, ½ of a boiled egg, and hot chili paste if desired.

Serves 4

*Broth can be prepared up to 2 days in advance and refrigerated until ready to use.

Make It a Soup Supper

This is a delicious dinner. We made a small investment in some chopsticks and those neat little Japanese soupspoons (they are plastic but still set the mood). Melon is sometimes considered a Japanese dessert, so serve **Bonus Recipe: Party Watermelon** *(pg. 85)* after the soup. This watermelon recipe brings us a little south of the border with a quick-cooking tequila syrup. It's a multi-cultural meal! Dessert is not required, but this is certainly refreshing.

Steak, Stout, and Spuds Soup

There are three reasons I adore this soup. The first one is practical; it's expensive to feed steak to a crowd, and this is very nice way to do just that without spending a fortune. Secondly, it's not so much fun to grill when it's cold or raining outside, and with rib-eye steak in the soup, no one will miss the smoke. Finally—and this is silly—I like the name (my initials, SSS). Best of all, your guests will feel pampered, as they should!

INGREDIENTS

1½- to 2-lb ribeye steak, trimmed and cut into bite-size pieces

1 tsp salt

1 tsp pepper

2 Tbsp olive oil, divided

2 Tbsp butter, divided

2 baking potatoes, peeled and cubed (small cubes for a soup bite)

½ onion, chopped

8 oz mushrooms, sliced

2 garlic cloves, minced

½ tsp thyme

½ tsp oregano

2 Tbsp flour

12-oz bottle stout or dark ale

6 cups beef broth

2 Tbsp tomato paste (the kind in a tube found in Italian section of grocery store is resealable)

Additional salt and pepper to taste

DIRECTIONS

(hint: To make this easier, chop everything that needs to be chopped first, and set aside.)

Heat together 1 Tbsp olive oil and 1 Tbsp butter in a Dutch oven or large pot over medium high heat.

Toss steak bites in salt and pepper.

Working in 2 batches, sauté steak very briefly, about 2 minutes total to brown; steak should still be rare on the inside.

Remove steak to a plate.

Add remaining olive oil and butter to the pan.

Cook potatoes and onions about 10 minutes until they begin to lightly brown.

Add mushrooms, garlic, thyme, and oregano, and cook another 2 minutes.

Stir in flour and cook for a minute, stirring constantly.

Pour in stout, stirring to keep lumps from forming.

Lower heat to medium and allow stout to bubble for about 5 minutes.

Stir in beef broth and tomato paste and simmer, uncovered, for 20 minutes to allow the soup to slightly thicken.

Taste and add salt and pepper as needed.

Remove soup from heat and stir in browned steak with any juices.

Allow soup to rest for 4 minutes to just heat steak through.

Serves 6

Make It a Soup Supper

Serve this with **Irish Soda Bread** *(pg. 94)*, right out of the oven, and cold beer of course. You could start the meal with a salad. **Peas and Crumbled Bacon Salad** *(pg. 61)* served on lettuce leaves fits the bill, and can be made at least a day ahead. It's such a filling, cozy dinner that I like to keep the mood going with a big plate of **Old Fashioned Tea Cakes** *(pg. 171)* for dessert.

White Bean Soup

If by chance you've baked the **Honey and Bourbon Glazed Ham** *(pg. 52)*, your reward is a marvelous ham bone that can be frozen to be used later for making this creamy, comforting soup. If not, don't worry; find a ham hock or even some deli ham at the grocery store. This soup is a Super Bowl tradition at our house.

INGREDIENTS

1 lb dried navy beans

3 carrots, diced into small pieces

3 stalks of celery, diced into small pieces *(hint: You can use celery leaves, finely minced, to add extra flavor.)*

1 small onion, minced

3 cloves garlic, minced

2 tsp olive oil

8 cups chicken or vegetable stock.

1 bay leaf

¼ tsp red pepper flakes (or to taste)

Meaty ham hock (reserved hambone with its remaining ham from **Honey Bourbon Glazed Ham** *(pg. 52)*, or about ¼ lb deli ham—not sliced, shred at the end of cooking)

Optional garnishes: thinly-sliced green onion and plenty of hot sauce

DIRECTIONS

Soak beans overnight in about 8 cups of water, or quick soak.* Drain.

Heat a large pot or Dutch oven over medium heat, and sauté vegetables in olive oil to soften, about 5 minutes.

Add beans and stock to the same pot.

Add bay leaf, red pepper flakes, and ham.

Bring the soup to a simmer, stir, and cover.

Simmer 3 to 4 hours, stirring occasionally and adding water if necessary.

About an hour before serving, remove ham, and shred meat, removing bone and any fat.

At this point, it's up to personal taste, but I like to either remove about a fourth of the beans and blend in the blender, or use a hand-held potato masher to achieve a creamy texture, not a puree.

Add ham back into the soup; remove bay leaf, taste for salt and pepper.

Serves 8 to 10

*Quick soak method: In a large pot, bring 6 to 8 cups of water with beans to a boil. Boil two minutes, cover, remove from heat, and allow to sit for an hour before proceeding with the recipe.

Make It a Soup Supper

Serve with **Bonus Recipe: Hot Water Cornbread** *(pg. 85)*. The cornbread is wonderful dipped in the soup, but served with a little honey butter it's also dessert! For honey butter, mix 4 Tbsp softened butter with 1 Tbsp honey. Add a cold beverage and you've got a Soup Supper that everyone will crave!

HONEY BOURBON BACON

Preheat oven to 375 degrees. Line a baking sheet with aluminum foil and place a baking rack* on top. Place 6 slices of bacon on the rack, being careful not to overlap. Bake for about 15 minutes, checking occasionally, until bacon is starting to get crispy in parts. Combine 3 Tbsp honey and 1 Tbsp bourbon in a small saucepan and bring to a boil. Brush honey sauce on bacon and sprinkle with a little black pepper. Bake another 5 to 8 minutes until bacon is crispy and dark. It will crisp as it cools. (By that I mean you get to taste a bite—then let it cool for guests.) Great for brunch too!

*Baking racks are inexpensive and very useful, but if you don't have one, crinkle up aluminum foil a bit to create ridges. Drain grease before brushing on the honey mixture.

PARTY WATERMELON

This makes a beautiful presentation. The recipe has tequila in it, but it does cook down so that very little alcohol is left. Cut one small, seedless watermelon into wedges. Simmer 1 cup of tequila with 1 cup sugar for 5 minutes until thick and syrupy. Cool with a mint sprig in the liquid, and spoon over the watermelon slices. Top with fresh mint and flaky salt. (My son adds hot chili powder!)

HOT WATER CORNBREAD

Bring 2 cups of water to boil in a small saucepan. Add 1 tsp of salt and gradually whisk in 1¼ cups cornmeal. Remove from heat. Refrigerate dough until cool and firm, 30 to 60 minutes. Roll into small balls and flatten to ½-inch thick circles. Heat 2 to 3 Tbsp canola oil in a nonstick or iron skillet over medium high heat. Fry corn cakes about 2 minutes per side until brown and crispy. Drain on paper towels and serve.

VIII
Eight Easy Breads

Here is the truth—we all love bread. People talk about how hard it is to bake bread, how long it takes, and how much patience is required to get it done. Well I disagree. My oven is about as reliable as my 10-year-old basset, and I don't have extra time or frankly enough patience to fill a thimble on a good day, but these recipes make baking fun, definitely easy, and oh so worthwhile.

Two of these bread recipes—**Irish Soda Bread** *(pg. 94)* and **Blue Cheese and Walnut Bread** *(pg. 90)*—don't even require a bread pan. The **Blueberry Buttermilk Lemon Loaf** *(pg. 91)* and **Banana Bread** *(pg. 89)* are chock full of fruits and nuts. **My Honey's Muffins** *(pg. 97)* feature our own back yard honey. Local honeys are great for baking. My son's hot pepper garden is the inspiration for **Sweet Jalapeño Cornbread** *(pg. 100)*.

When I say Eight Easy Breads, I mean it. Not one of these recipes will take more than a few minutes of prep time, and they definitely take less than an hour to bake. No special equipment is required except a muffin pan and, for a couple of the recipes, a bread pan. I did indulge in my fantasy of owning a mini-loaf pan. Now, if I decide to use that pan, I have eight little loaves of bread and I can give some away. That's another thing—nothing says you care about someone more than bringing them a loaf of fresh, homemade bread. Forget those expensive bottles of wine for hostess gifts, and start baking. A home that smells like fresh-baked bread is the one I want to be in. There's a party waiting to happen anytime bread comes fresh and hot out of the oven!

Banana Bread

My mother makes great banana bread. She inspired me to get some of those adorable little pans to make mini loaves. She adds nuts, or not, depending on what grandchild is dropping by and their preference. I like nuts, and I know my mom won't mind that I also added nutmeg and switched vanilla for a little bourbon. She taught me to experiment!

INGREDIENTS

1 stick butter (½ cup), softened	2 ⅓ cups flour
1 cup sugar	1 tsp baking soda
3 ripe bananas	½ tsp salt
2 eggs	½ tsp nutmeg
2 Tbsp bourbon	Optional: ¾ cup chopped pecans or walnuts

DIRECTIONS

Preheat the oven to 350 degrees.

Spray a loaf pan with cooking spray.

With an electric mixer, combine sugar and butter, and beat until light and fluffy.

Add bananas, and mix until bananas are combined with butter and sugar.

Add eggs and bourbon.

Mix in flour, baking soda, salt, and nutmeg until just combined.

Stir in nuts if desired.

Bake for 45 minutes until lightly browned and center is set.

*Will also make 12 muffins. Bake 25 minutes until set.

Serving Suggestion: Makes a well-appreciated gift if you bake an extra loaf!

Blue Cheese and Walnut Bread

Blue cheese and walnuts are a perfect pairing on a cheese plate, so why not bake them together and enjoy a beautiful loaf of warm bread?

INGREDIENTS

4 cups flour	2 oz blue cheese, crumbled
½ cup sugar	1 egg, beaten
1½ tsp baking powder	1½ cups buttermilk
1½ tsp baking soda	⅓ cup walnuts, chopped
1 tsp salt	1 Tbsp butter, melted for brushing loaf
½ stick butter (4 Tbsp), cut in pieces	

DIRECTIONS

Preheat the oven to 375 degrees.

Line a baking sheet with parchment paper, or spray with cooking spray.

In a large bowl, whisk together flour, sugar, baking powder, baking soda, and salt.

Add butter and, using your hands or a fork, mix until butter is almost combined.

Mix in nuts and cheese and stir to coat with flour mixture.

Stir in buttermilk and egg; dough will be loose.

Knead dough together on a floured surface (waxed paper for easy cleanup).

Form into a round and place on prepared baking sheet.

Cut an X on top with a serrated knife and bake for 40 to 50 minutes until golden brown.

Brush with melted butter.

Cool before slicing.

Serving Suggestion: Just like with a cheese plate, it's nice to enjoy this bread with a glass of chardonnay or a zinfandel. Pear slices make a pretty presentation.

Blueberry Buttermilk Lemon Loaf

This bread was inspired by a roadside stop for produce that featured blueberries too beautiful to resist. I may have accidentally bought more than necessary, and they were so delicious it would have been a shame to freeze them. So, what's a girl to do? Make bread of course. Buttermilk and lemon zest plus a lemon glaze make this extremely irresistible. Better bake two.

INGREDIENTS

6 Tbsp butter, softened (can do in the microwave, 6–8 seconds)

1 cup sugar

2 eggs

1 tsp vanilla

Zest of 1 lemon, save lemon juice for glaze (a cheese grater works to zest a lemon)

½ cup buttermilk

1½ cups flour (plus 2 Tbsp to coat blueberries)

1 tsp salt

1 tsp baking powder

¼ tsp baking soda

1 cup blueberries

Glaze

¾ cup powdered sugar

lemon juice

DIRECTIONS

Preheat the oven to 350 degrees.

Spray an 8 x 13 loaf pan with baking spray.

With an electric mixer, beat butter, sugar, and eggs.

Add vanilla, lemon zest, and buttermilk.

On low speed, mix in flour, salt, baking powder, and baking soda until just combined.

Toss blueberries with 2 Tbsp flour, and stir gently into batter.

Pour batter into prepared loaf pan and bake for 50 to 60 minutes until golden brown and set.

Allow bread to cool on a baking rack before removing it from the pan.

To make the glaze, combine about 2 Tbsp lemon juice from zested lemon with ½ to ¾ cup powdered sugar. Pour over cooled loaf.

Serving Suggestion: Delicious as part of a brunch menu and sweet enough to be dessert.

Ginger Biscuits

When English people refer to ginger biscuits, they mean a ginger cookie. These, howe   ally biscuits made with buttermilk and all the stuff that makes biscuits good. Ginger is a flavor that almost everyone adores, and biscuits are part of my heritage. They just belong together. A little butter is all you need to enjoy this delicious treat.

INGREDIENTS

¼ cup crystallized ginger (sometimes called candied ginger)

2 cups self-rising flour (see pg. 54 to make this flour if you don't have any)

1 tsp ground ginger

½ stick cold butter (4 Tbsp), cut in 4 pieces

2 Tbsp molasses or brown sugar

½ cup buttermilk (may need a little more if dough is too stiff)

Optional: 2 Tbsp Calvados or apple cider

DIRECTIONS

Preheat the oven to 400 degrees.

Line a cookie sheet with parchment paper, or spray with cooking spray.

Chop crystallized ginger into small bits by hand or in the food processor, and set aside to mix in last.

Either by hand or in the food processor, combine flour and powdered ginger and work in the butter.

Add molasses, buttermilk, and calvados or apple cider, and mix until just combined (don't over-mix).

Add more buttermilk if needed to make dough come together.

Mix in crystallized ginger.

On a floured surface (waxed paper for easy cleanup), roll dough to about a ¾-inch thickness.

Cut biscuits with a biscuit cutter (a glass works in a pinch), and place on prepared baking sheet.

Bake for 12 to 14 minutes until lightly browned.

Brush tops with melted butter if desired.

Makes 12 to 14

Serving Suggestion: These are great with a Soup Supper. Also, a perfect afternoon snack when you just need a little something.

Irish Soda Bread

This is a free-form loaf of bread, which means you don't even need a bread pan. The sweetness of the raisins and the unique flavor of caraway seeds make this bread something special. Warm bread is always a treat, and this one is so easy to make.

INGREDIENTS

4 cups flour	1 cup raisins
¼ cup sugar	1 egg
1¼ tsp baking soda	1¾ cups buttermilk
2 Tbsp caraway seeds	½ stick butter (4 Tbsp), melted
1¼ tsp salt	

DIRECTIONS

Preheat the oven to 350 degrees.

Lightly spray a baking sheet with cooking spray, or line with parchment paper.

In a large bowl, mix together flour, sugar, baking soda, caraway seeds, salt, and raisins.

In a small bowl, beat together egg and buttermilk, and stir in melted butter.

Add the buttermilk mixture to the dry ingredients in the large bowl.

Knead dough together to form a round loaf, and place on prepared baking sheet.

Cut an X on top of the loaf with a serrated knife, and bake for 45 to 50 minutes until it is lightly browned and sounds hollow when tapped.

Cool before cutting.

Serving Suggestion: This bread is great for toast the next day. Raisins and toasters can be a disaster, so use your oven or toaster oven. Also, it's nice to take to a friend.

Blue Cheese Walnut Bread (pg. 90)

The Honey Playlist

Honey Pie—The Beatles

Honey, Honey—ABBA

Honey Bee—Blake Shelton

Sugar Pie Honey Bunch—Four Tops

Tupelo Honey—Van Morrison

Wild Honey—The Beach Boys

American Honey—Lady Antebellum

Homegrown Honey—Darius Rucker

A Taste of Honey—Herb Alpert

Money Honey—Lady Gaga

American Money—BØRNS

Honey—Mariah Carey

A Taste of Honey—Barbra Steisand

My Honey's Muffins

We are new to the world of beekeeping. My husband does the hard work, but I pick the hive colors and cook with the honey. These are simple but beautiful little muffins. Fill a breadbasket with a batch for any occasion, and watch them "fly away."

INGREDIENTS

2 cups flour	1 cup whole milk (you can combine low-fat with half & half)
½ cup sugar	½ stick butter (4 Tbsp), melted
3 tsp baking powder	1 egg
⅛ tsp baking soda	¼ cup honey
½ tsp salt	

DIRECTIONS

Preheat the oven to 400 degrees.

Spray a 12-cup muffin pan or 24-cup mini muffin pan with cooking spray.

In a large bowl, mix together flour, sugar, baking powder, baking soda, and salt.

Combine milk, butter, eggs, and honey.

Add wet ingredients to flour mixture and stir to combine.

Pour batter in muffin tins ¾ of the way full and bake 12 to 15 minutes for regular size muffins, 10 to 12 minutes for minis.

Cool for a few minutes before removing from pan.

Serving Suggestion: Add ½ cup raspberries to the batter before baking. Delicious!

Stout and Maple Muffins

These are irresistible. I know this because when I said to my husband "you can have all you want," I wasn't thinking a full dozen. Luckily, they are easy to make (again). The muffin batter comes together in minutes, and you just pop the pan in the oven. Use a nice dark beer. Your kitchen will smell amazing. Neighbors may drop by unexpectedly!

INGREDIENTS

6 Tbsp butter, softened (can do this in the microwave 6 to 8 seconds)

¾ cup brown sugar

2 eggs

½ cup stout

½ cup sour cream

¼ cup maple syrup

1¾ cups flour

1 tsp baking soda

½ tsp baking powder

¾ tsp salt

Glaze

6 Tbsp powdered sugar

3 Tbsp maple syrup

1 to 2 tsp of the remaining stout

DIRECTIONS

Preheat the oven to 350 degrees.

Spray a muffin pan with cooking spray (or line with muffin cups).

Beat butter and sugar with an electric mixer until well blended.

Add the eggs, and mix to combine.

Turn off mixer to add stout, sour cream, and maple syrup.

Mix on low speed until just combined.

On low speed, add the flour, baking soda, baking powder, and salt, mixing until just combined.

Spoon batter into prepared muffin tins, filling them ¾ of the way full, and bake for 20 to 25 minutes.

Cool muffins and remove from pan before glazing.*

To make glaze, mix ingredients and slowly spoon over muffins. (If glaze is too thick, add a drop of stout or syrup.)

Makes 12

*Place on waxed paper or a baking rack before glazing for easy cleanup.

Sweet Jalapeño Cornbread

This recipe feeds a crowd but can be cut in half* and baked in an iron skillet for a great presentation. My son grows violently hot peppers, so I have to test them before I let him throw them in the batter. Jalapeños are generally pretty mild, but be brave and check one before baking so your guests won't have to "Drop It Like It's Hot," as the song goes.

INGREDIENTS

1½ sticks butter (12 Tbsp), softened (you can microwave 8 to 10 seconds)

⅓ cup sugar

3 eggs

2 cups buttermilk

2 cups cornmeal (not a mix)

1½ cups flour

4 tsp baking powder

2 tsp baking soda

1¼ tsp salt

4 to 5 fresh jalapeños, seeded and chopped (fresh really makes a difference)

DIRECTIONS

Preheat the oven to 400 degrees.

Spray a 9 x 13-inch baking dish or large iron skillet with cooking spray.

With an electric mixer, combine butter and sugar until light and fluffy.

Beat in eggs, and add buttermilk.

Add cornmeal, flour, baking powder, baking soda, and salt, and mix until just combined.

Stir in chopped peppers.

Pour batter into prepared dish and bake for 30 to 35 minutes until lightly browned.

Cool 5 minutes before cutting.

*If you cut the recipe in half, use 2 eggs.

Makes 24 squares

Serving Suggestion: Cornbread and soup belong together. This is also wonderful with the **Barbeque Turkey Breast** *(pg.24)* or as side dish with *Chilaquiles (pg.47)*

IX
Nine Notable Side Dishes

In the South, side dishes are as important as the entrée, hence the term "meat and three," with the "three" of course being the side dishes. Luckily rolls, biscuits, and cornbread don't count.

Most of us who like to cook for family and friends wouldn't dream of attempting three side dishes with a meal. It's not that the idea lacks merit—it lacks a cafeteria-style set up that includes several professional-grade dishwashers and cooktops, plus more people to boss around than your husband, wife, romantic interest, or roommate. But a fabulous side dish can absolutely be what takes a dinner from "that's nice dear" to "exceptional!"

Chicken from France *(pg.140)* just needs those **Mashed Potatoes with Roasted Garlic and Buttermilk** *(pg.110)* to achieve perfection, and **Flank Steak and the Perfect Marinade** *(pg.143)* is begging to be served with **Couscous with Almonds, Raisins, and Roasted Vegetables** *(pg.107)*. I can't say enough about what a marvelous combination **Spice-Rubbed Pork Tenderloin** *(pg.154)* is with **Brown Sugar and Bourbon Carrots** *(pg.104)*.

See what I mean? The combinations are endless and oh so much fun to imagine. Go ahead and get those **Swor House Baked Beans** *(pg.114)* started, then pat out the burgers, put on the dogs, and pop open a beer. A party is just about to happen.

Brown Sugar and Bourbon Carrots

It's amazing how confusion in the kitchen can result in a new favorite dish. I was cooking dinner for friends and asked my husband to pick up some asparagus on the way home. The asparagus was to be a last-minute preparation; everything else was ready to go. The asparagus didn't make it, and nothing else was available in any quantity to serve as a vegetable except a bunch of fancy tri-colored carrots. Here is a ten-minute dinner-saving side dish that you will fall in love with.

INGREDIENTS

1½ lb carrots, peeled and sliced in ½ inch rounds (tri-color are pretty, but not necessary)

3 Tbsp butter, divided

⅓ cup bourbon

⅓ cup brown sugar

½ tsp salt (or more—it really brings out the taste)

½ tsp pepper

Optional: 2 Tbsp chopped chives

DIRECTIONS

Melt 2 Tbsp butter in a skillet over medium high heat.

Add carrots, and stir for a minute to distribute butter.

Turn heat to medium and add bourbon.

Cook for a minute to let bourbon begin to evaporate, then stir in the brown sugar.

Cover the skillet and lower heat to barely a simmer.

Allow carrots to cook for 5 to 7 minutes, stirring a couple of times.

Uncover, add salt and pepper and remaining 1 Tbsp of butter, and allow glaze to thicken 2 to 3 minutes.

Top with chives if desired and serve.

Serves 8

Serving Suggestion: Great with the **Spice-Rubbed Pork Tenderloin** *(pg. 154)*

Cheese Pudding

This is as elegant as a cheese soufflé, but will never let you (or itself) down. Serve it to impress; eat it because it's yummy.

INGREDIENTS

½ stick butter (4 Tbsp), softened   ½ tsp garlic salt

8 to 10 slices of firm white bread   ¼ tsp dry mustard

8 oz grated sharp cheddar cheese   ¼ tsp cayenne pepper

4 eggs   2 tsp Worcestershire sauce

2 cups milk

DIRECTIONS

Butter an 8-cup capacity baking dish.

Cut crusts off of bread and lightly butter one side.

Place half of the bread, buttered side up, in the casserole.

You may need to cut one piece in half to fill casserole.

Cover with half of the cheese and top with remaining pieces of buttered bread.

Top with the remaining cheese.

In a mixing bowl, whisk together the remaining ingredients—eggs, milk, salt, mustard, pepper, and Worcestershire sauce—and pour over the bread.

Let the casserole rest, covered, in the refrigerator for an hour before baking, or up to a day.

Preheat the oven to 350 degrees.

Bake until the top is puffy and browned, about 45 minutes. Cool slightly before serving.

Serves 6

Church Supper Squash

I've never been to a potluck supper that didn't have a marvelous squash casserole. This one is a favorite.

INGREDIENTS

2 lb yellow squash (4 or 5 medium), sliced in one-inch pieces

½ onion, chopped

1 tsp salt

1 cup Parmesan cheese

1 cup mayonnaise

2 eggs

½ tsp garlic salt

1 tsp pepper

½ cup cracker crumbs

1 Tbsp melted butter

DIRECTIONS

In a large saucepan, boil squash, onion, and 1 tsp salt in water to cover until squash is very tender, about 15 minutes.

Drain thoroughly in a colander, pressing down with a spoon to remove excess liquid.

Preheat the oven to 350 degrees.

Spray an 8 x 8 or similar size baking dish with cooking spray.

Mash squash and onion together with a fork or potato masher, and beat in Parmesan cheese, mayonnaise, eggs, garlic salt, and pepper.

Pour squash mixture in prepared casserole.

Mix cracker crumbs with butter and sprinkle over the casserole.

Bake for 30 minutes.

Serves 8, easy to double

Serving Suggestion: To change this casserole, sharp cheddar can be a substitute for Parmesan, and add 2 Tbsp canned jalapeños or one fresh jalapeño, minced.

Couscous with Almonds, Raisins, and Roasted Vegetables

My friend Emily and I have made this together for a few cooking classes. I thought I'd better write it down because we both talk the whole time we cook, so its highly likely no one but us has any idea what we're saying. This dish never fails to impress, and we always have a blast. Now here's what to do!

INGREDIENTS

2 Tbsp butter

2 cloves garlic, minced

3 cups chicken or vegetable stock

1½ cups dry couscous

½ cup slivered almonds, toasted

¼ cup raisins

1 Tbsp olive oil

1 large red pepper, diced in one-

inch pieces

1 zucchini, sliced in rounds

1 onion, sliced

1 can chickpeas, drained and dried

½ tsp salt

½ tsp pepper

Optional: any other veggies you like—asparagus or squash, use what you have

DIRECTIONS

Preheat the oven to 450 degrees.

Line a roasting pan with foil for easy cleanup.

Melt butter in a large saucepan over medium heat.

Add garlic and sauté until just beginning to brown.

Add chicken stock and bring to a boil.

Remove from heat, add the dry couscous, stir, and cover for 10 minutes.

Coat foil lined pan with olive oil, add vegetables, and toss with salt and pepper.

Roast in the oven for 15 minutes or until lightly browned, stirring every 5 minutes.

To serve, stir almonds and raisins into couscous.

Place couscous on a large serving platter and top with roasted vegetables.

Serves 8

Make It a Meal

Try this with **Flank Steak and the Perfect Marinade** *(pg. 143)*. It also works as a wonderful meatless meal all by itself.

Roasted Asparagus with Easy Hollandaise Sauce

I have a friend who claims she married her husband because he made hollandaise sauce on their first date. People think it's the hardest thing to do, but it's so easy and takes less than a minute to make—really! Once you discover this, the world is your oyster. Hollandaise sauce is the basis for eggs Benedict. It's excellent with a grilled steak, and good on so many other vegetables, like squash, zucchini, and roasted Brussels sprouts. Try it for dipping artichoke leaves with **Bonus Recipe: Steamed Artichokes and Hollandaise Sauce**. It's divine!

INGREDIENTS

2 pounds asparagus

1 Tbsp olive oil

1 tsp salt

Easy Hollandaise Sauce

3 egg yolks (room temperature is better, but if you forget and need them last minute, put eggs in a bowl of warm water for 5 minutes)

3 Tbsp fresh lemon juice

1 tsp salt

¼ tsp cayenne

¼ tsp paprika

9 Tbsp butter (1 stick plus one Tbsp), melted

DIRECTIONS

Preheat the oven to 450 degrees.

Line a baking pan big enough to spread out asparagus with foil for easy cleanup.

Put asparagus in pan, drizzle olive oil over asparagus, and sprinkle with salt.

Spread asparagus out in the pan to roast.

Roast for 10 to 12 minutes until beginning to brown but still crisp tender.

For sauce, add egg yolks, lemon juice, salt, cayenne, and paprika to the jar of a blender.

Melt butter (can use microwave, but make sure butter is very hot).

While the butter is melting, blend egg mixture for about 15 seconds.

With blender running, slowly pour in hot butter and blend for about 30 more seconds until sauce is thick.

The sauce can stay in the blender up to an hour and can be re-heated if needed by quickly blending in 2 tsp hot water for a couple of seconds.

Remove to a serving plate and top with hollandaise sauce.

Sauce: Makes about 1½ cups

Asparagus: Serves 6 to 8

Serving Suggestion: Top each serving of asparagus with a poached or fried egg. Add some crusty bread to soak up the sauce, and enjoy a lovely meatless meal.

Fill a large pot that holds a steamer with about 3 inches of water, place steamer in pot, and add a lemon cut in half to the steamer. Bring water to a boil. Prepare artichokes by using kitchen scissors to cut off the tips (pointy parts) of the outer leaves. Use a sharp knife to cut off about 1 inch off the top of the artichokes, then rinse the artichokes in cold water. Place into steamer and cook for 30 to 40 minutes until leaves pull off easily. Drain and serve with hollandaise sauce for dipping leaves. For a treat, pull out fuzzy part in the center and enjoy the artichoke heart underneath.

Mashed Potatoes with Roasted Garlic and Buttermilk

Everyone has that one dish that is the ultimate comfort food. You crave it whether you're sick, sad, or celebrating. For me, it's mashed potatoes. I could eat them for every meal and never regret it. If necessary, I will eat a restaurant's mediocre version but will always be wishing for these. Don't say you weren't warned!

INGREDIENTS

4 lb potatoes, peeled and cut into large chunks (Yukon Gold make great mashed potatoes)

1 head garlic, top sliced off

½ tsp olive oil

1 Tbsp salt for boiling potatoes

10 Tbsp butter (1 stick plus 2 Tbsp), cut in cubes

1 cup buttermilk

½ to 1 cup half & half or whole milk

2 to 3 tsp salt (more to taste)

1 tsp pepper

DIRECTIONS

Preheat the oven to 350 degrees.

Place cut garlic head on a piece of aluminum foil, drizzle with olive oil, and wrap foil around garlic.

Bake the garlic for about 45 minutes; remove from oven, open foil, and let cool.

Fill a large saucepan with cold water; add potatoes, 1 Tbsp salt, and bring to a boil.

Lower heat and simmer about 15 to 20 minutes until potatoes are fork-tender.

Drain potatoes in a colander, and mash with a potato masher, ricer, or with a fork. (Use what you have, but try to get most of the lumps out.)

As soon as potatoes are mashed, stir in butter to melt.

Squeeze cooled garlic cloves from their skins and mash in with potatoes.

Add buttermilk and half & half or milk, adding more if necessary to get a creamy consistency.

Add salt and pepper, taste for seasonings.

Serves 8 to 10

Serving Suggestion: When you are hosting a dinner, mashing potatoes while your guests look on is not a very pleasant activity. You can make this recipe ahead of time, put the potatoes in a casserole dish, and dot with about 2 tsp of butter cut in tiny pieces. The potatoes go in the oven at 350 degrees about 20 minutes before dinner is served. This may bother some mashed potato snobs, but one taste and that won't be a problem.

Red Beans and Rice in a Slow Cooker

My love affair with New Orleans will never end. I was in college when I first visited and had Red Beans and Rice three times in one weekend. There was hardly time to slip in a beignet. This can definitely be a main dish, but we always serve **Red Beans and Rice** with **New Orleans Barbequed Shrimp** for a crowd (see below). It's so easy but so perfect.

INGREDIENTS

1 lb dried red beans, rinsed and drained

½ lb Andouille sausage, thinly sliced

¼ lb smoked ham (deli), leftover ham, or ham hock

1 onion, chopped

1 bell pepper, chopped

3 ribs celery, chopped

5 garlic cloves, chopped

2 bay leaves

2 Tbsp paprika*

1 tsp onion powder

1 tsp garlic powder

1 tsp dried basil

1 tsp dried oregano

1 tsp dried thyme

1 tsp black pepper

Hot sauce to taste (start with 5 or 6 drops)

6 cups chicken or vegetable broth

To serve: cooked rice, according to package directions

Optional garnish: green onions, thinly sliced

*Ingredients from paprika through black pepper can be substituted with 1 to 2 Tbsp Creole seasoning. It won't be quite the same, but you can play around with it.

DIRECTIONS

Combine all ingredients except rice in a 4-quart slow cooker.

Cook on high 7 to 8 hours until beans are tender.

Optional: I like to remove 1 cup of beans and mash with a fork, then return to pot.

Shred ham to make bite-size pieces and return to pot.

Serve over cooked rice with plenty of hot sauce to pass.

Serves 8 to 10

Serving Suggestion: On a busy day, start this in the morning, and by dinnertime you have a perfect dinner of **Red Beans and Rice**. Quick-cooking rice makes it a breeze.

Make It a Meal

Invite a lot of people to dinner and start a pot of **Red Beans and Rice** that morning. Cook **New Orleans Barbeque Shrimp** from the "You're Grown" blog when your company comes—it takes about 15 minutes. A loaf of crusty bread is fine, but if you have time, whip up **Sweet Jalapeño Cornbread** *(pg. 100).* Some New Orleans beer would be a welcome addition. TheDeerOne.com/recipes

Southern Fried Corn

Growing up, we ate fried corn all the time. In the winter, when the corn wasn't as good, we sweetened it up with a pinch of sugar. That's the best! It's sort of like caramelized corn when it's cooked that way. Restaurant menus feature grilled corn and street corn, but surprise company with this and they'll be hooked. Corn on the cob will never be the same!

INGREDIENTS

8 ears of corn

½ stick butter (4 Tbsp)

1 Tbsp sugar

1 tsp salt

1 tsp pepper

¼ cup cream or half & half

Optional: 1 tsp fresh thyme

DIRECTIONS

Peel away the outer layers and pull off the silk from each ear of corn.

Holding corn upright in a bowl, carefully cut away the kernels so they fall in the bowl.

Once all the kernels are removed, scrape the edges of each piece of corn, holding it over the bowl to remove any corn liquid (milk).

Melt butter in a large iron skillet or nonstick pan over medium high heat.

Add corn, spreading kernels evenly across the skillet.

Lower heat to medium, and cook, stirring once or twice to keep corn from sticking.

Stir in sugar, salt, and pepper, and let corn begin to lightly brown on one side.

Stir again and add cream.

Cook another 1 to 2 minutes, stirring up any browned bits.

Sprinkle in thyme if you are using it.

Serve immediately!

Serves 6 to 8

Make It a Meal

Try this with **Homemade Chicken Tenders** *(pg. 122)*, or **Simple Homemade Sausage** *(pg. 46)*, plus **Buttermilk Biscuits** *(pg. 54)*, and fresh sliced tomatoes for a perfect summer feast.

The Swor House Baked Beans

This is the original "no official recipe required" recipe. I like to add ground sirloin, change up the beans, and toss in a bit of bell pepper, depending on what's available. Don't hesitate to play with your food!

INGREDIENTS

1 (28-oz) can baked beans, undrained

1 (15-oz) can dark red kidney beans, drained

1 (15-oz) can black beans, drained

1 cup frozen lima beans or 1 (15- oz) can of lima or butter beans, drained

1 (15-oz) can diced tomatoes, undrained

1 small onion chopped

¾ cup ketchup

½ cup brown sugar

2 Tbsp sorghum or molasses

2 tsp salt (taste—beans have varying levels of salt)

½ tsp garlic salt (more to taste)

¼ tsp red pepper flakes

Optional: 6 slices of bacon for topping

DIRECTIONS

Preheat the oven to 350 degrees.

In a large casserole, combine all ingredients except bacon.

Top the filled casserole with bacon, cut to fit if desired.

Bake for 1 hour, checking a couple of times.

If beans still have too much liquid after 1 hour, bake another 20 minutes to half hour.

Serves 12 to 15

Serving Suggestion: Great for any cookout, potluck supper, or **Barbeque Picnic** *(pg. 24)*. Can be baked in a disposable foil pan for a picnic, and wrapped in heavy foil.

X
Ten Top Appetizers

Appetizers have always been an essential part of entertaining. After all, the word itself means food and drink to stimulate the appetite. How perfect is that? No matter what kind of party you are hosting, you will find these recipes are not only easy to make, but will also delight any gathering of friends and family. In fact, this book is chock-full of delicious appetizers that will keep your company entertained. The ten appetizers in this chapter are also complemented by so many more, like the **Garlic and Curry Candied Pecans** *(pg.16)* and the **Tiny Cheese Biscuits** *(pg.18)*. And remember the whole section on **Picnic Sandwiches**? Sandwiches cut into cocktail size bites, like **Cream Cheese, Olive, and Pecan** *(pg.41)* or **Classic Chicken Salad** *(pg.37),* are a delightful and tasty nibble.

Cocktail parties with yummy appetizers are a wonderful way to entertain a lot of people without having to worry about serving dinner. Everyone loves a Friday night cocktail party. People can stop by after a long day, enjoy the company of friends and maybe make a new one, have a drink and a bite to eat, and head home for the weekend. It's fun to make one signature cocktail ahead of time, and then let your guests serve themselves, making whatever drink they like from the ingredients at the bar. (See the list for a well-stocked bar pg.5). That way, you won't be running around trying to get drinks for everyone instead of enjoying your guests. I feel the same way about the food. Appetizers that can be done ahead, like **Sallie's Rosemary Parmesan Crisps** *(pg.127)* and **Spinach and Sausage Balls** *(pg.128),* are perfect. Both can be made ahead and simply pulled out of the freezer to go in the oven before guests arrive. A snack on the bar like **Firecrackers** *(pg.121)* is always a nice touch. A bite-size sandwich is a great option as well. For that kind of party, 4 or 5 appetizers are plenty, counting on 3 or 4 bites a person per appetizer.

For a dinner party, one appetizer is always enough, and here's the best part—it's ok to run out. Your guests will be having a marvelous meal and you don't need them to come to the table already full. Try to serve a pickup appetizer unless you don't mind tons of dirty dishes! **Stick Cheese** *(pg.129)* is a favorite here.

If your appetizers are for an event—for example watching a Sunday afternoon football game or celebrating a birthday—a few of those sandwiches mentioned before would be perfect. The **Beer-Steamed Shrimp** *(pg.118)* can be served for a quick tasty bite. The **Stuffed Eggs** *(pg.130)* will disappear before you can grab one if you aren't quick enough.

When enjoying a comfortable evening with a few friends, let appetizers be dinner. The **Warm Cheese and Beer Dip** *(pg.132)* is one of my favorite things to serve. The **Homemade Chicken Tenders** *(pg.122)* is my son's favorite recipe when he throws a party. Tell everyone to bring a favorite bottle of wine and your evening is set.

On a final note, you don't have to make everything. Cheeses, olives, and nuts are at all grocery stores and are always welcome to the party. Good chips and veggies with a dip are easy to serve. My last resort but favorite snack in a quick minute is popcorn, of course. The whole point of a party is to have fun and to enjoy your guests. Now go do that!

Beer-Steamed Shrimp with Spicy Cocktail Sauce

You know it's a party when shrimp is on the menu. This is a cinch to prepare and makes for one gorgeous presentation. My kid has made this cocktail sauce since he could reach the kitchen counter. Even then I had to watch him with the hot sauce!

INGREDIENTS

2 lb large shrimp, peeled and deveined

2 Tbsp olive oil

½ onion, sliced in rings

1 head garlic, cut in half

¼ tsp red pepper flakes

12 oz dark beer (lager)

2 sprigs fresh thyme (½ tsp dried)

3 Tbsp Old Bay Seasoning

2 lemons cut in half

Richard's Spicy Sauce

½ cup ketchup

Juice of ½ a lemon

1 Tbsp horseradish sauce

½ tsp hot sauce

DIRECTIONS

Heat oil over medium high heat in a pot large enough to hold shrimp.

Add onion and garlic, and cook until just soft and starting to brown, about 5 minutes.

Add red pepper flakes and stir to combine.

Pour in beer and cook for a minute or two to heat.

Stir in 3 cups of water, thyme, Old Bay Seasoning, and the lemon halves.

Bring to a boil, lower heat, and add shrimp.

Simmer about 5 minutes, until shrimp are firm and pink.

Drain in a colander, reserving onion, garlic, thyme, and lemon halves as part of the garnish, and transfer to a serving bowl.

Mix together spicy sauce.

Eat shrimp warm, or chill in the refrigerator.

Serves 8 as an appetizer

Firecrackers (aka Hot Puppies)

This is a recipe for **Firecrackers**, sometimes known as Hot Puppies. This first happened at a recent out of town cocktail party where everyone kept saying "Have you tried these Hot Puppies?" But here at home they are still Firecrackers. This recipe is the result of tinkering around with a ridiculously expensive mix for spicy crackers that I was given, and the unfortunate lack of a functioning oven when an immediate appetizer was required. This is a Sallie Special. Everyone wants these **Firecrackers** for parties, and the good news is that really anyone can make them. They are as easy as can be. Five minutes of prep is probably overkill, and they are very inexpensive. **Firecrackers** are sure to be the first disappearing act from the table! They are barking good.

INGREDIENTS

1 box (4 sleeves) of saltine crackers

1¼ cups canola oil

1 package of ranch style dip or dressing mix

1½ to 2 Tbsp red pepper flakes
(depends on how hot you like them)

Large plastic container or resealable baggie,
big enough to hold all ingredients

DIRECTIONS

Put crackers in container of choice.

Mix all other ingredients and pour over crackers.

Shake gently for a minute or two, trying not to break crackers.

Repeat, shaking every 10 minutes or so a couple more times for optimal spicy distribution.

They're ready, but they're even better the next day and will last for several days tightly sealed.

Homemade Chicken Tenders

One day my son came home from elementary school excited because he had two chicken fingers and nine tater tots for lunch. He explained that the lunch ladies counted your tater tots at the end of the cafeteria line because nine was the limit. Well, that's a weird way to teach math and science. Why nine? When did chickens get fingers? And what is the lesson about nutrition here? I grew up with real fried chicken. It had bones but no fingers, so it's taken awhile for me to come around to what has thankfully been re-named chicken tenders. Fast food versions are pretty awful, but since Nashville has become known as "The Hot Chicken City," we have more options. Still, I believe anyone can make the very best chicken tenders in their own kitchen and never crave a to-go fix again! You can even make it hot! Your friends are going to love this! It's perfect for a potluck, a picnic, watching a ball game, or having a casual dinner.

INGREDIENTS

1½ lb thinly sliced chicken breasts (*hint: They come packaged that way at the grocery store, or you can buy chicken breasts and cut and pound them to about ¾-inch thickness.*)

2 cups buttermilk

2 Tbsp salt

1 Tbsp sugar

2 garlic cloves, smashed

Juice of 1 lemon

Hot sauce

2 cups cornstarch

2 cups panko or breadcrumbs

1 cup flour

1 Tbsp salt

1 Tbsp paprika

2 cups canola or vegetable oil

DIRECTIONS

(hint: This recipe is much easier if you bread the chicken about 30 minutes before you plan to pan-fry it. You can even pre-bread the chicken and freeze it until you suddenly crave fried chicken.)

To make the marinade, in a large bowl combine 2 cups buttermilk, 2 Tbsp salt, 1 Tbsp sugar, 2 cloves smashed garlic, juice of 1 lemon, and 5 or 6 drops of hot sauce.

Add chicken to marinade ingredients and marinate for an hour or up to 3 hours.

Cover a baking sheet with foil or waxed paper.

Place cornstarch on one plate, and panko mixed with flour, salt, and paprika on another. *(hint: For easy clean up, I keep inexpensive paper plates around for jobs like this.)*

Remove chicken from marinade, reserving marinade, and dip each piece one at a time in cornstarch, then back in marinade, and then in panko mixture.

Place coated chicken on prepared baking sheet and refrigerate at least 15 minutes.

Heat oil in a large iron skillet or nonstick skillet over medium heat until a panko or bread crumb sizzles. (If oil is too hot, chicken will burn before the center cooks. It's not a bad idea to cook one piece first to test the oil.)

Fry two or three pieces at a time, checking to make sure pieces don't get too brown.

Drain chicken tenders on paper towels.

Serves 6 to 8 hungry people

Make it "Nashville Hot"

In a small bowl, mix 1 Tbsp paprika, ½ tsp sugar, 1 tsp salt, ½ tsp turmeric, and 2 tsp cayenne pepper. (You can play around with the spices to make it hotter or milder.) When chicken has cooked, mix 3 Tbsp of the leftover hot oil into the spices. Brush this mixture on chicken tenders and let it melt into the crust. Prepare to sweat!

Make It a Meal

Now you have a great recipe for fried chicken. Make **Bonus Recipe: Buttermilk Waffles** and there you have it—Chicken and Waffles.

Mix 1½ cups flour, 1 Tbsp sugar, 1 tsp salt, 1 tsp baking powder, and ½ tsp baking soda in a large mixing bowl. Mix 6 Tbsp melted butter, ¾ cup buttermilk, ¾ cup milk, and 1 egg together, and add to dry ingredients. Cook in a waffle iron according to directions. *Makes 4 large waffles*

Oscar Night Popcorn

My son is a movie fanatic in a way that not many people understand. Oscar night represents the pinnacle of watching nearly every movie for a year—funny, tragic, scary, biographical, dramatic, futuristic, and even foreign. The point of this is that our Oscar night menu has to be a spectacular reflection of the year's best films. It may follow a few themes or cuisines, but some years the nominations are all over the place—a little bit of everything. So I made this popcorn a little bit of everything (bagel).

INGREDIENTS

3 tsp caraway seeds

2 tsp flaky sea salt (can use kosher salt)

1 tsp each black and white sesame seeds

1 tsp poppy seeds

2 tsp granulated garlic

¼ cup canola oil

¾ cup popping corn (I prefer white kernels)

½ stick butter (4 Tbsp), melted

DIRECTIONS

Toast caraway seeds in a small skillet on medium high heat, shaking the pan for about a minute.

Add seeds to a small bowl.

Add salt and use a pestle or the back of a spoon to crush the seeds and salt.

In the same skillet, toast sesame seeds, shaking the pan for about a minute, or until white seeds start to turn golden.

Add to the small bowl, and stir in poppy seeds and granulated garlic.

Add oil to a large pot with a lid, and add the popcorn kernels.

Cover and cook over medium high heat until corn starts to pop.

Cook, shaking pan until corn stops popping—about 4 minutes.

Pour popped corn in a large serving bowl and toss to coat with butter.

Add the seasoning and toss again. *You'll* be the winner!

Serving Suggestion: Keep this seasoning on hand; it's good on lots of things. I even use it to perk up steamed green beans!

Roasted Red Pepper Hummus

When I go to a party, I'm always happy to see a dip that really is finger food so I can grab a bite without all the effort of trying to balance a plate while holding a glass. When I host a party, I like to have a healthy option that's still utterly delicious and makes a gorgeous presentation. This is it. The red peppers give the hummus a new twist and delicious flavor; a little lemon juice keeps it bright. It tastes so much better and actually is so much better than the stuff you can buy at the store. The fact that it can be made a day before the event and pulled right out of the fridge makes it perfect for a party. Served with crisp, beautiful veggies, it's usually the first dish to disappear at any party.

INGREDIENTS

1 cup chopped jarred roasted red peppers (or 2 red peppers roasted*)

2 cloves garlic, peeled

2 (15-oz) cans chickpeas (garbanzo beans), drained and rinsed

3 Tbsp lemon juice

⅓ cup tahini (sesame paste—can be found in most grocery stores in Greek or Mediterranean sections)

¼ cup olive oil

1 tsp salt

Small pinch of cayenne pepper

DIRECTIONS

Combine all ingredients in a food processor or blender until well blended and the mixture is smooth (taste for salt).

Cover and chill until serving time; best served at room temperature. (A drizzle of olive oil over the top is a nice touch before serving.)

Makes about 2 cups

*To roast your own peppers, move the oven rack close to the broiler. While the broiler preheats, core the peppers and cut into large, flat pieces. Broil the peppers 5 to 8 minutes until the skin is charred. Cool for a minute, then seal peppers in a plastic bag to steam, and let them cool to room temperature before using them in a recipe.

Serving Suggestion: Possibilities for dippers include, carrots, radishes, celery, peppers, black olives, sliced squash and zucchini, cherry tomatoes, even crackers—you'll find your favorites!

Sallie's Parmesan Rosemary Crisps

Sallie's Rosemary Parmesan Crisps

This is without any doubt my most popular and most requested recipe. Here it is for anyone to make and enjoy. What was a lucky culinary accident for me (doesn't cornstarch look like powdered sugar to anyone else?) has turned into my very favorite cocktail appetizer, hostess gift, and popular addition to any gathering. Rosemary Parmesan Crisps are always expected at my house. I keep a roll of dough in the freezer at all times. There's one there right now.

INGREDIENTS

2 cups flour

1 cup powdered sugar

1 Tbsp rosemary leaves (a nice long, fresh stalk is great, but dried works too)

½ tsp salt

½ tsp black pepper

½ cup grated Parmesan cheese

2 sticks butter (1 cup), cut into 1-inch pieces

DIRECTIONS

Add flour, sugar, rosemary, salt, pepper, and Parmesan to the bowl of a food processor and pulse to combine. (An electric mixer works too.)

Add butter, and pulse until soft dough forms.

Place one sheet of plastic wrap on a flat surface.

Place the dough on plastic wrap, using the wrap to shape the dough into a log approximately 2 inches in diameter.

Chill until firm, about an hour. (Or be impatient like me and put it in the freezer for 30 minutes.)

Preheat the oven to 375 degrees.

Line a baking sheet with parchment paper, or spray with cooking spray.

Slice dough into ¼ inch slices and arrange about 1 inch apart on baking sheet.

Bake 10 to 12 minutes until edges begin to brown.

Cool 5 minutes and move to wax paper to cool. Store in airtight container.

Makes about 36

Serving Suggestion: The dough keeps in the freezer for up to a month tightly wrapped in plastic.

Spinach and Sausage Balls

For years we've loved Spinach Balls as an appetizer, and then one day I thought, why not add sausage? I did, and the rest is history. It's a perfect marriage that will last forever!

INGREDIENTS

1 (8-oz) package breakfast sausage, cooked, crumbled, and drained (can use **Simple Homemade Sausage** *(pg. 46)*)

2 (10-oz) packages frozen chopped spinach, thawed and cooked (can do this in the package in the microwave)

1 (16-oz) package herb stuffing (usually in the baking aisle)

3 sticks butter (1½ cups), melted

4 eggs

1 onion, chopped

1 tsp garlic salt

1 tsp salt

3 Tbsp black pepper (more or less to taste)

DIRECTIONS

Preheat the oven to 350 degrees.

Line a cookie sheet with parchment paper or spray with cooking spray.

Mix all ingredients in a large bowl.

Roll into balls slightly smaller than a Ping-Pong ball, and place on a cookie sheet.*

Bake for 15 to 20 minutes until starting to brown.

Serve warm, but they're delicious at room temperature too.

Makes 50 to 60

*At this point you can freeze the **Spinach and Sausage Balls** on the cookie sheet and put them in a large, freezer-safe resealable baggie. They can be cooked straight from the freezer or saved for an emergency appetizer!

Stick Cheese—That Needs a New Name

When I was a newlywed, I came up with this clever little cheese spread using brie cheese, my husband's favorite. I served it at a party, and my husband took a bite, smiled, and said it was "mighty tasty"—his highest praise. I overheard a guest ask him what was in the cheese spread and was extremely entertained to hear my husband say, "Some kind of cheese and some yummy little sticks." He is more rosemary savvy by now…I think. But the name stuck.

INGREDIENTS

8-oz wedge of brie cheese, rind mostly removed, slightly softened

1 stick butter (½ cup), slightly softened

¼ cup slivered toasted almonds

1 tsp pepper

2 Tbsp fresh rosemary (1 Tbsp dried)

DIRECTIONS

Combine cheese and butter in the bowl of a food processor or in a mixing bowl.

When the mixture is well combined, add almonds, pepper, and rosemary, and pulse or lightly mix to combine without pulverizing nuts or rosemary.

Place mixture in a serving bowl and refrigerate until ready to use.

Serve with crackers.

Serving Suggestion: Serve this with a little hot pepper jelly from the "You're Grown" blog on the side. This could also be one of the spreads for a **Bruschetta Picnic** *(pg.26)*. It keeps for at least a week in the refrigerator. TheDeerOne.com/recipes

Stuffed Eggs

No cocktail party or cookout is really complete without stuffed eggs, at least in this part of the country. We've always called them stuffed eggs, not deviled eggs. It may be a regional thing, or it may be because they are just delicious and not a bit devilish. I've invited people to parties who ask if stuffed eggs will be there. I guess they'll always be the most popular kid at the party.

INGREDIENTS

12 eggs, boiled*

1 to 2 Tbsp sweet pickle juice

⅓ cup mayonnaise (more if needed, for consistency)

½ tsp salt (or ¼ garlic salt and ¼ regular salt)

¼ tsp pepper, or to taste

Optional: paprika to sprinkle over the top

Garnishes: sliced olives are traditional, but some other options are capers, chives, crunchy bacon pieces, smoked salmon, or even caviar for a really fancy party

DIRECTIONS

Slice cooled, peeled eggs in half, and scoop yolks into a mixing bowl.

Mash egg yolks thoroughly—a fork will do the trick, but a ricer can make it speedy.

Combine mashed yolks with mayonnaise, pickle juice, salt, and pepper.

Fill egg whites evenly with a generous mixture of filling, either by spooning it into each egg white, or by putting the yolk mixture into a large baggie, pressing it all down to the bottom, and cutting a small hole in the tip of the baggie to pipe filling into egg whites.

Top with a sprinkle of paprika and the garnishes of choice.

You don't need a special egg plate to make a pretty presentation; any platter or dish you like will be just fine.

Makes 24

How to hard-boil an egg—*(pg. 39) (hint: I always boil a couple of extra eggs in case one doesn't peel well or cracks. You can use the yolks from extra eggs in the filling.)*

Warm Cheese and Beer Dip

This dip is a favorite at a restaurant we have loved for years in the Smoky Mountains. I wish we could go there all the time, but we can't, so here is my version. We like it even better because we make our own dippers and serve it piping hot. Plus, the drive to the grocery is a bit easier than to the mountains.

INGREDIENTS

2 cups white American cheese (If you can't find it, ask at the grocery store deli.)

½ cup half & half

½ cup dark beer

½ tsp garlic salt

½ tsp dry mustard

½ tsp Dijon mustard

1 Tbsp Worcestershire sauce

A few drops of hot sauce

DIRECTIONS

Preheat the oven to 350 degrees.

In a double boiler, melt the cheese with the half & half.

In a small bowl, mix beer and remaining seasonings.

132

Using a wire whisk, stir the beer mixture into the melted cheese.

Pour cheese into individual ramekins or into one large one.

Bake for 20 minutes until bubbly.

Serve with any or all of the following: pretzels, French bread, sausages, grilled steak or chicken, veggies, and apple or pear slices. Let your imagination run wild! Delicious!

Serves 6 as an appetizer

Serving Suggestion: Sometimes we purchase pizza dough and cut it into long pieces, season with garlic salt, and bake to use as dippers for the **Warm Cheese and Beer Dip**. I won't deny that this has been served as a casual supper on many a chilly night!

XI
Eleven Elegant Entrées

Even though this chapter features eleven excellent entrées, perfect for entertaining, I could never realistically have narrowed the number of entrées to eleven. There are too many wonderful choices, so I snuck in recipes for amazing entrées all throughout this book. You'll find marvelous recipes that work as entrées in the sections for soups, sides, appetizers, picnics, and brunches.

These eleven main dishes are absolute favorites—perfect party foods equally delightful for entertaining a crowd, a family dinner, a cozy evening with friends, or a dinner for someone special. You will find that all of these entrées are paired with ideas for side dishes and desserts, and sometimes salads, appetizers, and cocktails. Realistically, no one has the time to prepare elaborate meals that require hours of work in the kitchen. Truly, even if I had the time, I lack the patience and suspect many people feel the same way. These menus are easy enough so that you can host without needing to jump up to serve courses or finish cooking something. Your guests can be relaxed and you will be too.

A delicious crowd pleaser that works equally well for a special dinner is **Weekend Shrimp Pasta** *(pg. 156)*. This fabulous meal, made all in one pot, is a cinch to prepare even after a busy day. A simple salad and a loaf of bread round out the menu, and the dinner feels like a celebration! For a night at the grill, two delicious choices are **Flank Steak with the Perfect Marinade** *(pg. 143),* which will feed a hungry group, and **Seared Tuna with Romesco Sauce** *(pg. 147),* featuring a simple blender sauce that makes it a beautiful and elegant dish to present to company.

Buffet-style is an easy way to host a party. Every guest can help themselves to what they want, and the mood is casual. **Italian Flag Lasagna** *(pg. 145)* is perfect for that kind of dinner. The **Bonus Recipe: Perfect Garlic Cheese Bread** *(pg. 158)* and **Tiramisu for Beginners** *(pg. 182)* make the meal special. It's likely that with little or no encouragement, your guests will be returning for seconds and thirds.

If you feel like having friends over for a get-together but time for cooking is a problem, go for the **Slow Cooker Roast Pork Taco Bar Party** *(pg. 152)*. Start your roast in the slow cooker, and then go about your busy day, stopping on the way home to grab tortillas, salsa, chips, and the ingredients for the **Beer Float** *(pg. 160)*

For a special dinner, when I want to really impress but do so with ease, **Chicken Marsala** *(pg. 141)* is an absolute favorite, with buttered angel hair pasta on the side. Add your pick from the dessert section and maybe that **Bonus Recipe: Rebujito** *(pg. 159)*. No matter how you choose to serve them, all of these entrées are designed to be both easy and delicious, and are recipes that will become your go-to party dishes and family classics. Your company will love them, and the compliments will be yours to collect. Most importantly, these recipes are planned to give you time to enjoy your guests and enjoy the dinner you have served, and perhaps even enjoy a festive beverage in the process. That's what makes it a party—good food, good friends, and you, the most fabulous host.

Bolognese Sauce for Every Day

Spaghetti is sacred in our family. It is a first-night dinner in any rental vacation house. It's Sunday night supper when we are getting ready for the week ahead, and it's comfort food when someone needs comforting. When I announced that I was messing around with the basic spaghetti sauce we've enjoyed for years, it did not go over well. I talked about Northern Italy, the richness of the meat sauce, and the wine with a touch of cream, and got the look that means don't do it. But I did, and we all agree that this is the best pasta sauce we have ever tasted. This Bolognese sauce with pasta is perfect for a party. Best of all, it doesn't require hours of simmering to get a deep rich flavor. The ingredients do the work, making it the ideal recipe to prepare anytime. Serve it for a big party, a family dinner, or to somebody you love. If this recipe had a fortune cookie it would say, "Candles and wine make this dinner divine."

INGREDIENTS

2 Tbsp olive oil

½ onion, finely chopped

1 carrot, finely chopped

6 cloves of garlic, finely chopped (can make fine chopping easy by cutting the veggies into big pieces and using a few pulses of the food processor)

1 lb lean ground beef sirloin (I like sirloin, but you can substitute turkey.)

1 tsp oregano

¼ tsp red pepper flakes

1 cup red wine

1 (28-oz) can crushed tomatoes

2 Tbsp tomato paste (If you can find it in a tube in the Italian food section of the grocery, it's easier to use small amounts.)

1 tsp sugar (or to taste—it cuts the acidity in the tomatoes)

2 tsp salt

¼ cup heavy cream

½ tsp nutmeg

Optional: fresh basil, chopped (3 or 4 Tbsp)

To serve: 12 oz cooked pasta of choice and grated Parmesan cheese.

DIRECTIONS

Heat olive oil in a large Dutch oven or pot over medium high heat.

Add onion, carrot, and garlic and sauté until just softened, about 2 minutes.

Add meat, and cook for about 5 minutes until it loses the pink color, breaking up meat with a spoon as it cooks.

Stir in the oregano and red pepper flakes, and then add in the wine.

Cook for a minute, stirring to scrape up any browned bits.

Add tomatoes, tomato paste, sugar, and salt.

Simmer for about 15 minutes while you prepare the pasta.

To finish the sauce, add cream, nutmeg, and half of the basil if desired, and simmer for 10 minutes more.

Stir drained pasta into sauce and top with grated Parmesan and reserved basil. If this is a party, serve from a pretty bowl or casserole dish, and allow guests to help themselves. Have extra cheese on hand.

Serves 4

Make It an Occasion

A crowd favorite appetizer, **Sallie's Rosemary Parmesan Crisps** *(pg. 127)* is lovely to offer before this meal. Put out a tray of those and watch them disappear. It's hard to go wrong with wine when serving pasta, so open a couple of your favorite reds. The **Bolognese Pasta** is so nice to serve with **Bonus Recipe: Perfect Garlic Cheese Bread** *(pg. 158)* and a salad. **Bonus Recipe: Spinach and Artichoke Heart Salad** *(pg. 11)* is one of the easiest in the world, and one of the best. A perfect dessert with this Italian themed menu would be the **Tiramisu for Beginners** *(pg. 182).*

Cheddar Biscuit and Beef Pot Pie

My nephew hosted an exchange student from Australia named Seb, and so we all called him Seb the Australian. I'm not sure why just Seb wouldn't do, but somehow the name stuck. I got to spend some time with Seb the Australian on a trip to the Smoky Mountains. He described in great detail his favorite dish from home, and my recipe, he claimed, nailed it. Of course, in all honesty, who doesn't love a big casserole with beef and potatoes, particularly one topped with cheese biscuits (although he thought the word biscuit meant dessert; that one took some explaining)? This makes a large casserole and feeds a crowd. To me, it's more interesting and much more delicious than shepherd's pie. Seb the Australian agrees.

INGREDIENTS

2 Tbsp butter

2 baking potatoes, peeled and cubed

1 onion, chopped

2 carrots, peeled and sliced

2 cloves garlic, chopped

1 Tbsp fresh thyme (1 tsp dried)

1 Tbsp fresh rosemary (1 tsp dried)

1 Tbsp fresh parsley (1 tsp dried, or omit)

2 lb ground beef

1½ tsp salt

1 tsp pepper

3 Tbsp flour

2 cups milk

1 cup beef or chicken broth

Optional: 2 Tbsp sherry

1 cup frozen green peas

Biscuits

2½ cups self-rising flour

1 stick (½ cup) cold butter, cut in cubes

1 cup grated sharp cheddar cheese

1 cup buttermilk (more if needed)

DIRECTIONS

Melt 2 Tbsp butter in a large pot or Dutch oven over medium heat.

Add potatoes, onion, and carrots, and sauté until softened, about 8 minutes.

Stir in thyme, rosemary, and parsley, and transfer to a bowl.

In the same pot, cook ground beef over medium high heat, breaking into pieces until browned. (Remove any accumulating liquid as the beef cooks.)

Return vegetables to the pot with the beef and stir in salt and pepper.

Add 3 Tbsp flour and cook 2 minutes, stirring constantly.

Add milk and broth, and cook to thicken sauce, about 5 minutes, stirring occasionally.

Add sherry if desired, and green peas.

Put meat mixture in a 9 x 13 or similar size dish deep enough to hold meat and biscuits.

Preheat the oven to 350 degrees.

For biscuits, I use my food processor, but it is quite easy to do this by hand in a bowl.

Blend flour, butter, and cheese to combine.

Add buttermilk, and mix to form dough.

Roll out dough and cut into biscuits, re-rolling leftover pieces.

Place biscuits on top of the sauce, pushing them in a little.

Bake for 30 minutes until casserole is bubbly and biscuits are browned. *(hint: If biscuits are browning too quickly, place a piece of aluminum foil lightly over the casserole.)*

Serves 8 to 10

Make It an Occasion

Assemble the casserole ahead of time and bake it when guests arrive. It contains lots of veggies and, of course, biscuits, but if you want to serve a salad as well, keep it simple. Look for a mix of cabbage and kale in the precut salad section at the grocery. Mix with olive oil, lemon juice, salt, pepper, and a small amount of honey. Add toasted almonds and cranberries. The salad can be prepared an hour ahead and rest in the fridge. I quickly learned that Australians love chocolate. Make **Best Chocolate Chip Cookies** *(pg. 169)*. If serving Australians, call them biscuits.

Chicken from France

In my younger days, when I was living in an apartment with roommates, we thought this recipe was the height of sophistication. It involved mixing mustard and maple syrup, garlic and herbs. We called it **Chicken from France**, and pretended that it was Julia Child's recipe. It wasn't, but guys loved it, plus we could pool our money and collectively afford the ingredients to feed a small crowd. Recently, I cooked this for friends and noticed a fairly refined gentleman lick his plate! I call that a compliment you don't want to forget!

INGREDIENTS

10 to 12 skinless, boneless chicken thighs (usually 5 or 6 in a package)

1½ tsp garlic salt

⅔ cup mustard, whatever you have on hand

⅔ cup maple syrup (real)

2 Tbsp rice wine vinegar (sort of a mild flavor; you can substitute another vinegar if you don't have it)

4 to 6 cloves garlic, minced

4 tsp fresh rosemary, chopped (it really is good, but dried will work, just use ½ as much)

¼ tsp cayenne pepper

DIRECTIONS

Preheat the oven to 450 degrees.

Spray a casserole dish large enough to hold the chicken with cooking spray.

In a small bowl, combine mustard, maple syrup, vinegar, garlic, rosemary, and cayenne pepper.

Add chicken to the casserole, and sprinkle with garlic salt and pepper.

Pour sauce over chicken.

Bake for 40 to 45 minutes, spooning sauce over the chicken a couple of times during baking.

Be sure to serve chicken with the delicious sauce. Oh la la!

Serves 8, very easy to double

Make It an Occasion

Mashed Potatoes with Roasted Garlic and Buttermilk *(pg. 110)* are perfect for soaking up all of this delicious sauce, but if you are pressed for time, rice is an easy side dish and also delicious. A salad is always a nice touch—for this menu try **Bonus Recipe: Arugula Salad with Pears, Red Onion, and Honey Vinaigrette** *(pg. 158)*. For dessert, what could be better than the **Upside-Down Fruit Cobbler** *(pg. 183)?*

Chicken Marsala

This recipe is hands down the most requested chicken dinner in our house. It takes only thirty minutes to prepare from fridge to table, requires one pan, and is marvelous with pasta or all alone. It sounds fancy and tastes it too. **Chicken Marsala** is an excellent choice to impress company or a date. The chicken is incredibly tender after you pound it. You feel great because all of your aggression went into chicken pounding and you know you have a marvelous meal ahead of you. The last order of business is to open a bottle of wine (maybe a pinot noir) and light the candles.

INGREDIENTS

4 chicken breasts (*hint: Chicken breasts at the grocery seem to have grown over the last few years—2 large ones cut in half length-wise like opening a book will make four servings.*)

¾ cup flour

2 tsp salt

1 tsp pepper

2 Tbsp olive oil

2 Tbsp butter, divided

8 oz sliced mushrooms

2 cloves garlic, minced

1 tsp fresh sage, chopped (¼ tsp if dried)

¾ cup Marsala wine

¾ cup chicken broth

¼ cup heavy cream

DIRECTIONS

Preheat the oven to 200 degrees.

Put chicken pieces in a large, resealable baggie and pound, using a meat mallet or rolling pin, to about ¼-inch thickness.

Add flour, salt, and pepper to the baggie, and shake to coat chicken.

In a large skillet, melt butter and oil over medium high heat.

Shake chicken pieces to remove excess flour, and sauté until golden brown on each side, about 4 minutes per side.

Remove chicken to a heat-proof dish, cover with aluminum foil, and place in oven to stay warm.

Add remaining Tbsp of butter to the same skillet, and sauté mushrooms until they begin to brown, about 3 minutes.

Add garlic and sage, and sauté another minute.

Add Marsala, scraping the skillet to incorporate any browned bits.

Add broth, and simmer to reduce, about 5 minutes.

Add cream and return chicken to the sauce.

Cook for 3 minutes more, until sauce is thick and chicken is coated.

Serve over pasta of choice if desired. *(hint: Start boiling water for pasta when you begin to sauté the chicken.)*

Serves 4, easy to double and keep chicken warm in the oven

Make It an Occasion

Serve with angel hair pasta mixed with a little butter and fresh parsley and a lemon slice on the side. A simple green vegetable, asparagus or broccoli steamed in the microwave, is a perfect accompaniment. A light and refreshing after-dinner cocktail, **Bonus Recipe: Rebujito** *(pg.159)* would be a delightful after-dinner treat! Serve with **Honey and Lavender Icebox Cookies** *(pg.170)* for a light and perfect sweet touch.

Flank Steak and the Perfect Marinade

A marinated, grilled flank steak can be your best friend for serving a crowd. The secret is the marinade. The best part is the leftovers. A good friend said this recipe was all the reason anyone needed to own this cookbook.

INGREDIENTS

2 lb flank steak

1 Tbsp fresh ginger *(hint: Grate ginger with a lemon zester or cheese grater. You can buy ginger in a squeeze tube in the produce section of many groceries.)*

2 cloves garlic, crushed

½ cup sherry

2 Tbsp hoisin sauce (Find in Asian section of the grocery store.)

2 Tbsp sesame oil

¼ cup brown sugar

⅛ tsp red pepper flakes

DIRECTIONS

Mix together marinade ingredients in a large bowl or in a large, resealable baggie.

Score flank steak lightly on both sides with a sharp knife to help absorb flavor.

Add flank steak to baggie and marinate for at least 2 and up to 12 hours in the refrigerator.

To cook the steak, heat a grill pan, broiler, or outdoor grill until very hot.

Remove steak from marinade and pat dry with a paper towel.

Generously salt and pepper both sides of the steak.

If you are using a grill pan, oil lightly with canola oil.

Cook steak for 3 to 4 minutes per side (rare) to 7 to 10 minutes (well done) on each side.

Remove steak to a carving board and let it rest 10 minutes (steak absorbs the juices during this time).

Slice the steak against the grain for much more tender pieces.

End pieces will be more done and the middle section rarer, so your guests can select their favorite.

Serves 6 to 7

Serving Suggestion: Use leftovers to top **Tomatoes, Potatoes, and Green Bean Salad** *(pg. 66)* Delicious for a summer supper or picnic!

Make It an Occasion

For a grilled dinner, **Stuffed Eggs** *(pg. 130)* are a nice appetizer to pass and easy to prepare ahead of time. Serve grilled flank steak with **Couscous with Almonds and Roasted Vegetables** *(pg. 107)*, easy to prepare while the steak rests. Since you've got the grilling spirit going, why not try **Bonus Recipe: Grilled Peaches with Ice Cream** *(pg. 160)* for dessert?

Italian Flag Lasagna

Why? Because it's red, white and green. Everyone needs a perfect lasagna recipe for entertaining. Here you go! It has beef and sausage—the perfect marriage.

INGREDIENTS

Sauce

2 Tbsp olive oil

1 large onion, chopped

4 cloves garlic, minced

1 lb sweet Italian sausage (can use turkey sausage)

1 lb ground beef (can substitute ground turkey)

1 (28-oz) can whole tomatoes

1 (6-oz) can tomato paste

1 tsp dried oregano

1 tsp dried basil

¼ tsp red pepper flakes

2 tsp salt

2 tsp sugar

½ cup red wine

Optional: Parmesan cheese rind (remove before using sauce)

One package lasagna noodles cooked according to package directions

Filling

1 (15-oz) container ricotta cheese

1½ cups mozzarella cheese, grated (divided in half)

1 cup Parmesan cheese, grated (divided in half)

1 egg

1 clove garlic

1½ cups fresh spinach

1 tsp salt

DIRECTIONS

Heat olive oil over medium heat in a large skillet or Dutch oven.

Add onions and cook until soft, about five minutes.

Add garlic, and stir for a minute more.

Add sausage and beef, breaking them up with a large spoon and cooking until no longer pink.

Stir in un-drained tomatoes, tomato paste, oregano, basil, pepper flakes, salt, sugar, wine, and Parmesan rind if you use it.

Simmer sauce, uncovered, for 20 to 30 minutes, stirring occasionally and breaking up tomatoes.

While the sauce is simmering, combine all ingredients for the filling in a food processor or blender, reserving half of the mozzarella cheese and half of the Parmesan cheese. (Or mix by hand, making sure to mince garlic and chop spinach very finely.)

Preheat the oven to 400 degrees.

Ladle one-third of the meat sauce into a lasagna pan or a 9 x 13-inch baking dish.

Spread the sauce evenly, and cover with one-fourth of the lasagna noodles.

Top with half of the filling and cover with another one-fourth of lasagna noodles.

Spread the noodles with another one-third of sauce and top with one-fourth of the noodles.

Top noodles with the remaining filling and top filling with the rest of the noodles.

Top the lasagna with the rest of the sauce and sprinkle reserved cheese over the top.

Bake, uncovered, for 35 to 45 minutes until sauce is bubbling.

Allow to cool for a couple of minutes before serving.

Serves 8

Make It an Occasion

Offer an easy make-ahead appetizer like **Stick Cheese** *(pg. 129)* with crackers and a couple of wine choices, a red and a white. A big salad is all you need with this meal, but **Bonus Recipe: Perfect Garlic Cheese Bread** *(pg. 158)* is always a hit. For dessert, it's almost impossible to resist **Chocolate Swirl Cheesecake Bites** *(pg. 166)*. Make them ahead and watch your guests swoon when you bring them out after dinner.

Seared Tuna with Romesco Sauce

The secret is the sauce. Romesco Sauce is delicious with so many things—chicken, meat, vegetables—and it takes 30 seconds to make. When you taste it, you'll know!

INGREDIENTS

6 tuna steaks, about 4 to 6 oz each and about 1-inch thick
(hint: You can substitute another fish. Mahi mahi or swordfish are good choices.)

2 Tbsp olive oil

Salt and black pepper

Romesco Sauce

2 jarred roasted red peppers (found with pickles in the grocery store, sometimes in Italian section)

½ cup almonds

1 slice bread (day-old stale is best)

2 Tbsp red wine vinegar

1 Tbsp honey

1 tsp paprika (smoked is great if you have it)

1 clove garlic, peeled

½ cup olive oil

1 tsp salt

½ tsp pepper

DIRECTIONS

Combine all ingredients for Romesco Sauce in a blender or food processor and process until smooth.

Pour sauce in a serving bowl and cover until ready to serve.

Heat grill or sauté pan over high heat.

Rub fish with olive oil, and sprinkle with salt and pepper.

If you are using a sauté pan for cooking fish, add 1 Tbsp of canola oil.

Cook tuna on grill or in sauté pan for about 2 minutes per side for rare interior; if you are cooking another fish, add extra time and cook until flakey and at your desired degree of doneness.

Serve with Romesco Sauce.

Serves 6

Make It an Occasion

This meal just cries out for grilled or pan-roasted veggies to dip in all of that lovely sauce. Good choices are asparagus, squash, zucchini, peppers, onions, and even okra. Drizzle with a little olive oil and sprinkle with salt first. **Bonus Recipe: Tabouli** *(pg. 160)*, my son's recipe, is a great side dish because it can be made ahead of time. A chilled rosé is a nice accompaniment. For dessert, the **Brown Sugar Chess Pie** *(pg. 165)* will send everyone home happy.

Shrimp and Chicken Enchiladas with Poblano Sauce

If my son's friends are coming over for dinner, there is about a 90-percent chance they'll want Mexican food. We all love tacos and the basic enchilada, but this recipe is a fabulous way to create a more elegant take on a Mexican menu. It seems like a lot of ingredients, but actually, you just use one pan to cook everything and one casserole dish for baking. This can be assembled several hours earlier and baked at party time. It feeds a crowd, and as my friend says, "it's shrimp scrumpdidleyumtious!" (Not sure about pronunciation)

INGREDIENTS

Filling

2 cups chicken breast, cooked and diced

2 Tbsp olive oil

1 lb shrimp, peeled and deveined (cut in half if large)

½ tsp salt

½ tsp pepper

½ onion, diced

2 cloves garlic, diced

2 Tbsp diced poblano pepper, seeds removed (reserve the remaining pepper for the sauce)

2 cups baby spinach

1 tsp cumin

1 tsp salt

4 or 5 dashes of hot sauce (to taste)

Juice of ½ a lime (reserve the other half for sauce)

½ cup Monterey Jack cheese, grated

12 flour tortillas

Sauce

½ stick butter (4 Tbsp)

½ cup diced poblano (reserved from filling ingredients)

4 Tbsp flour

2 cups chicken broth

1 cup sour cream

1½ cups Monterey Jack cheese, grated

Juice of ½ a lime

1 tsp salt (taste for seasonings— chicken broth salt levels differ)

DIRECTIONS

Put diced chicken in a large bowl.

Heat 1 Tbsp olive oil in a Dutch oven or large pot over medium high heat.

Toss shrimp with salt and pepper, and sauté for about 3 minutes until just pink. (Shrimp will continue to cook when enchiladas are baked.)

Add cooked shrimp to the bowl with chicken.

Add remaining olive oil to the same pan, and sauté onion, garlic, and poblano pepper for about 3 minutes.

Add spinach and cook for a minute to wilt.

Stir in cumin, salt, hot sauce, and lime juice.

Add vegetable mixture and ½ cup cheese to the bowl with the shrimp and chicken.

For sauce, melt butter over medium high heat in the same Dutch oven or pot.

Add diced poblano pepper and cook for 1 minute.

Whisk in flour, and cook for 1 to 2 minutes until flour just starts to brown.

Gradually whisk in chicken broth, stirring for 2 to 3 minutes to thicken.

Add in sour cream and 1½ cups cheese, stirring to melt.

Add lime juice and salt, and taste for seasonings.

To assemble, preheat oven to 350 degrees.

Spray a 9 x 13 or similar size casserole dish with cooking spray.

Fill a tortilla with about ½ cup of the shrimp and chicken mixture.

Roll up, placing the tortilla in casserole seam side down.

Repeat with remaining tortillas.

Pour sauce over the tortillas.

Bake 30 to 40 minutes until sauce is bubbly and starts to brown.

Serves 6 to 8

Make It an Occasion

This one is easy. Start with a pitcher of margaritas and your favorite chips and salsa. Served on romaine lettuce or red cabbage leaves, the easy make-ahead **Bonus Recipe: Black Bean and Corn Salad** *(pg.160)* is a beautiful side dish. Include **Peach Crisp** *(pg.178)* for dessert. Rave reviews are yours.

Peach Crisp (pg.178)

Slow Cooker Roast Pork Taco Bar Party

This is the perfect way to throw a party, even on a busy day. Here's how: get your roast ready for the slow cooker with the garlic and the rub the night before, and refrigerate it. Start it early the next day in the slow cooker and go about your business. Stop by the store to pick up taco bar ingredients—flour and/or corn tortillas, salsa, chips, maybe beer and ice cream for **Bonus Recipe: Beer Float** *(pg. 160)*, limes, sour cream, cheese, and toppings (the salad bar is your friend for chopped green onions, tomatoes, and radishes, even olives). Come home, finish your roast, put out Taco Bar ingredients, and get a good playlist going.

INGREDIENTS

5 to 8 lb Boston butt or pork shoulder (bone-in)

8 to 10 cloves of garlic peeled

3 Tbsp paprika

3 Tbsp brown sugar

2 Tbsp garlic salt

1 tsp cayenne pepper (more or less depending on your heat preference)

DIRECTIONS

Cut slits in the roast and insert garlic cloves.

Mix together paprika, brown sugar, garlic salt, and cayenne pepper, and rub over pork.

Put pork roast in a slow cooker set on High.

After about 6 to 8 hours, remove roast, and pour off all accumulated liquid.

Return roast to slow cooker set on Low.

After about two more hours you can remove the bone and shred the meat a bit to get more browned bits.

Depending on the size of your roast, it should be perfectly cooked in 10 to 12 hours.

For extra crispy pieces, place shredded roast pork on a foil-lined baking sheet and place under the oven broiler on high, stirring occasionally until desired brownness is achieved.

Serve the roast from a casserole dish and let guests make tacos with their choice of topping. Put topping in bowls, including lettuce, cheese, tomatoes, onions, cilantro, jalapeños, lime, guacamole, salsa, sour cream, and hot sauce.

Serves 12 at least!

Make It an Occasion

Start the party with plenty of chips and salsa and margaritas. For serving you might include **Black Bean and Quinoa Salad** *(pg. 161).* Make it the day before. For easy cleanup and a fun activity, cover your table with craft paper, and put out crayons. You might end up owning a masterpiece, slightly spotted with salsa! My son and his cohorts insist that a **Bonus Recipe: Beer Float** *(pg. 160)* is the perfect dessert for this party.

Bonus Recipe: Beer Float

Spice-Rubbed Pork Tenderloin with Blue Cheese Butter

Marinate the pork and make the butter a day ahead, and your very elegant dinner is ready in no time at all. This is a dinner to impress your date, your boss, even your mom!

Spice-Rubbed Pork

INGREDIENTS

2 to 3 lb pork tenderloin	1 tsp garlic salt
1 cup apple juice concentrate, thawed	1 tsp salt
1 cup chicken broth	1 tsp cumin
1 cup bourbon	¼ tsp cayenne pepper
3 Tbsp paprika	2 Tbsp canola oil
3 Tbsp brown sugar	

DIRECTIONS

Combine apple juice, chicken broth, and bourbon in a large baggie, and add pork tenderloin.

Marinate for at least 1 hour and up to 8 hours.

Preheat oven to 400 degrees.

Remove pork from marinade and pat dry.

In a small bowl, mix paprika, brown sugar, garlic salt, salt, cumin, and cayenne pepper.

Coat pork thoroughly with spice mixture.

In a cast iron or ovenproof skillet, heat oil over high heat.

Sear pork on all sides to brown it, about 2 or 3 minutes per side.

Place skillet with pork in the oven and cook to desired doneness, about 10 to 15 minutes.

Let pork rest for another 15 minutes before slicing.

Top each serving with **Blue Cheese Butter***.

Serves 6 to 8

Blue Cheese Butter

INGREDIENTS

½ stick butter (4 Tbsp), softened (can be done very carefully in microwave—about 8 seconds)

2 oz blue cheese

1 Tbsp chives or green onions, finely chopped

½ tsp black pepper

DIRECTIONS

With an electric mixer or a food processor, combine butter and blue cheese
until smooth.

Add green onions or chives, and black pepper, and mix until combined.

On a piece of plastic wrap, roll butter into a log shape about one inch in diameter.

Chill until ready to use.

*Can be made ahead of time and frozen.

*Flavored butters can be wrapped and frozen for months. It makes a delicious sauce
   as it melts on any meat!

Make It an Occasion

It might be fun to offer a signature cocktail before dinner. **Bonus Recipe: Aunt Nancy's Mojitos**
(pg. 161), served with mixed nuts (warm in microwave with a sprig of rosemary for 30 seconds), would be a nice
way to start the party. **Brown Sugar and Bourbon Carrots** *(pg. 104)* and **Bonus Recipe: Black Bean
and Quinoa Salad** *(pg. 161)* are perfect sides. Prepare the salad ahead of time, and sauté the carrots while the
pork roasts. End with an easy and refreshing make-ahead **Frozen Lemonade Pie** for dessert *(pg. 174).*

Weekend Shrimp Pasta

This should just be named "Your Favorite Shrimp Dish," because it will be now. It's your secret weapon when you've had a busy week but would still like to enjoy dinner and the company of a few close friends. This entire recipe takes less than 30 minutes to prepare and cooks all in one pot. It's been my experience that everyone is so delighted to have **Shrimp Pasta** that they are happy to be assigned to bring bread, a salad, or even the wine. That's what I call easy entertaining.

INGREDIENTS

16 oz dried fettuccini or other favorite pasta

12 to 16 oz medium to large raw shrimp, peeled and deveined

2 Tbsp butter

Zest of 1 lemon (optional: could always add a squirt of lemon juice)

2 Tbsp olive oil

4 to 5 cloves garlic, minced

1 cup cherry tomatoes, halved

⅛ tsp red pepper flakes

1¼ cups white wine

½ cup mascarpone cheese

12 oz fresh spinach

Salt and pepper to taste

DIRECTIONS

In a large pot, boil water and cook pasta according to package directions.*

While pasta cooks, chop garlic and slice tomatoes.

When the pasta is done, pour it in a colander and carefully wipe the pan dry.

Return pan to medium high heat, melt butter, and add about ¼ of the chopped garlic and the shrimp.

Add a pinch of salt, plus lemon zest if desired.

Cook shrimp on both sides until pink and firm, about 5 minutes (less time if you use smaller shrimp).

Remove shrimp to a small bowl or plate.

Add olive oil, remaining garlic, tomatoes, and pepper flakes to the pot, and sauté until garlic starts to soften, about 3 minutes.

Add wine and reduce for a minute.

Return shrimp and pasta to the pot; add cheese, stirring to melt.

Add spinach to wilt as it gets stirred into the pasta.

Serve immediately—Parmesan cheese optional.

Serves 4 to 5 generously

*Spray pan with cooking spray before adding water for an easier time wiping it clean.

Make It an Occasion

Consider offering an appetizer plate with a couple of cheeses, crackers, and olives. All can be purchased days ahead. Wine and pasta go hand in hand, but a signature sangria like **Bonus Recipe: My Sister's Sangria** *(pg. 161)* might be a fun way to kick off the evening. Take my suggestion and assign salad and bread to guests. Since the salad and bread are not your responsibility, you may have time to make a marvelous homemade dessert; it's difficult to beat the **Flourless Chocolate Amaretto Cake** *(pg. 172)*, but if time is an issue, a sophisticated and different dessert is vanilla ice cream topped with fruit and drizzled with honey.

PERFECT GARLIC CHEESE BREAD

Preheat the broiler. Slice 1 loaf of French or Italian bread (13 to 16 oz) in half lengthwise. Place bread cut side up on a baking sheet (line with foil for easy cleanup). In a small microwave-safe dish melt 1 stick butter with 4 cloves minced garlic, ¼ tsp red pepper flakes, and ½ tsp salt. Stir in ½ tsp oregano. Spoon the butter mixture evenly over bread. Sprinkle bread with about ½ cup Parmesan, and broil. (hint: *Watch it carefully — it can burn very quickly.*) Remove from oven and sprinkle with parsley if desired. Slice in 1-inch pieces and serve!

ARUGULA SALAD WITH PEARS,
RED ONION, AND HONEY VINAIGRETTE

In a large salad bowl, toss 1 bag of pre-washed arugula with 1 pear cut in thin slices and ¼ red onion cut in thin slices Add ½ cup of toasted walnuts and ¼ cup crumbled blue cheese. Dressing: In a jar with a lid, combine 3 Tbsp honey, 4 Tbsp white wine vinegar, ½ cup olive oil, 1 tsp salt, and ½ tsp pepper. Shake and pour over the salad.

REBUJITO

For each cocktail, combine 2 oz Fino sherry and 4 oz lemon-lime soda. Add ice and top with a slice of lime.

GRILLED PEACHES WITH ICE CREAM

Cut 4 peaches in half. Remove the pit but leave the skin on. Brush peaches lightly with olive oil and place cut side on the grill. Grill until grill marks are visible and peach is softening, about 4 minutes. Flip peaches over and brush cut sides with a mixture of 2 Tbsp honey and 1 Tbsp bourbon. Grill another 4 minutes. Serve warm with ice cream.

TABOULI

Put 2 cups bulgur wheat in a large bowl and pour 2 cups of boiling water over it. Cover with a dishtowel and let stand 30 minutes. In a salad bowl, combine ½ cup chopped parsley, ¼ cup chopped mint, 4 thinly-sliced green onions, 1 cup chopped tomatoes, juice of 3 lemons, and ¼ cup olive oil. Stir in cooled bulgur and 1 tsp of salt. (Add more salt or lemon juice if desired.) Serve cold or at room temperature. Keeps several days in the fridge.

BLACK BEAN AND CORN SALAD

Combine 2 cans of black beans, drained and rinsed, with 2 cups fresh corn kernels (about 3 ears—really fresh corn doesn't need to cook for this salad), ¼ cup chopped red onion, 3 Tbsp lime juice, 2 Tbsp chopped cilantro, 2 Tbsp sugar, 2 tsp salt, 1 tsp cumin, and hot sauce to taste. (This can also be a dip for chips.)

BEER FLOAT

This is the best taco bar dessert. To make one **Beer Float**, pour ½ cup dark beer over a scoop of chocolate ice cream. Add a straw!

AUNT NANCY'S MOJITO

For each cocktail, put 2 Tbsp sugar in a tall glass, add juice of 1 lime and 4 or 5 mint leaves. Crush or muddle to dissolve sugar and bring out mint flavor. Add ice to the glass (crushed is nice but not necessary). Top with about ½ cup club soda or sparkling water, and 1½ oz white rum. Stir and garnish with a mint leaf.

BLACK BEAN AND QUINOA SALAD

Combine 1½ cups cooked quinoa (package directions) with 1 can black beans, drained and rinsed. Add the fresh kernels cut from one ear of corn; ½ each of onion and red pepper, chopped; and 1 avocado, cut in small cubes. In a jar with a lid, add the juice of 2 limes, 2 Tbsp olive oil, 1 tsp sugar, ½ tsp cumin, ½ tsp salt (more to taste), and 4 or 5 drops of hot sauce. Shake it up and pour over salad, stirring to combine. Optional: chopped cilantro.

MY SISTER'S SANGRIA

Combine 1 bottle dry red wine, 1 cup vodka, 1 cup Cointreau or triple sec, 1 cup ginger ale, 2 cups club soda or sparkling water, and 1 Tbsp sugar. Add diced fruit: 1 lemon, 1 lime, 1 orange, 1 apple, and ½ cup grapes, halved. Chill and serve over ice.

XII
Twelve Just Desserts

"Just desserts" is a funny little saying used to refer to someone getting what he or she deserves, either good or bad. The original quote contained the word desert, but I'm sticking with the spelling "dessert" and counting on my just reward being a good one—a delicious dessert. When people say they aren't "dessert people," I assume that they are either suffering from the debilitating effect of some horrible calorie restrictive diet plan or they are lying. Really, how can you not at least like dessert? I love all desserts. I'll even admit to liking fruit for dessert, but I like it even better with a buttery crust and some ice cream—**Peach Crisp** *(pg. 178)*.

When you serve any of these dessert recipes, I promise your lucky guests will be dessert people. This book has desserts for even the finickiest eaters; your gluten-free friends will adore the **Flourless Chocolate Amaretto Cake** *(pg. 172)*, as will anyone who loves rich, dense chocolate. Take your party on a walk down memory lane with an old-fashioned **Strawberry Shortcake** *(pg. 179)*. Only the taste surpasses the presentation. I really am a fruit lover, and the **Upside-Down Fruit Cobbler** *(pg. 183)* is always at the top of my list, with its five-minute prep time, minimal ingredients, and sensational taste. Plus, it can be served warm or room temperature, making it party perfect. If you are invited to dinner, offer to bring dessert. You'll be the hit of the party when you show up with **Blondies with Dark Roots** *(pg. 164)* or **Mini Marscapone Cupcakes with Berry Glaze** *(pg. 177)* or both!

I find that people crave **Frozen Lemonade Pie** *(pg. 174)* all year long. It's such an easy dessert to serve— just pop it out of the freezer and listen to the contented sighs from the crowd. Just like the **Tiramisu for Beginners** *(pg. 182)*, which takes ten minutes to prepare, and then goes straight into the fridge, ready for you to serve whenever it's time for dessert. Then there are **The Fab Four** *(pg. 168)*: four amazing cookies that must be in your cookie jar. They are perfect for picnics and parties, and for giving to a friend in need. Enjoy looking through this chapter to find your favorite Just Desserts. Or better yet, find that they are all your favorites!

Blondies with Dark Roots

No, this does not refer to me (thanks to my good friend and hair dresser), but it is about my favorite dessert to take to any occasion. Cut it into little squares, and watch everyone go back for seconds and thirds. In the world of desserts, this is fairly irresistible.

INGREDIENTS

2 sticks butter (1 cup), softened (can do in the microwave in 8 to 10 seconds)

2 cups brown sugar

2 eggs

½ tsp salt

1 tsp vanilla

1 Tbsp bourbon (Secret revealed! Jack Daniel's preferred, but it's optional)

2 cups flour

1 cup chocolate chips

1 cup pecans, chopped and lightly toasted (toast in microwave about 30 seconds to a minute)

DIRECTIONS

Preheat the oven to 350 degrees.

Spray a 9 x 13-inch baking pan with cooking spray or line with parchment paper to make it easy to remove blondies.

With an electric mixer, beat together butter and brown sugar (can be done by hand).

Add eggs, salt, vanilla, and bourbon.

Stir in flour to combine.

Mix in chocolate chips and pecans.

Pour into prepared pan and bake for about 30 minutes until edges are golden brown and center is set.

Cool and cut into squares.

Makes 24 generous squares

Brown Sugar Chess Pie (The Mexican Pie Lie)

This spectacular recipe, shared by a friend, will always be called Mexican Pie in our house. My son forgot to tell me he had invited friends over for dinner, but when he did, I whipped up a fast casserole of enchiladas. He asked what was for dessert, and I didn't miss a beat before saying Mexican Pie. I mean for heaven's sake, what is a chess pie but a flan in a crust? (well, maybe with a little—or a lot—more butter). So that's what I made, Mexican Pie, aka **Brown Sugar Chess Pie**. *Sí, muy bueno*!

INGREDIENTS

2 Tbsp flour

1 cup brown sugar

½ cup sugar

1 stick butter (½ cup), melted

2 eggs, beaten

½ cup half & half

1 tsp vanilla

¼ tsp salt

1 unbaked pie shell (purchased or make your own*)

DIRECTIONS

Preheat the oven to 375 degrees.

Whisk first eight ingredients together in a large bowl.

Pour into an unbaked pie shell.

Bake for 35 minutes or until pie center is set. (It will be puffy when it comes out of the oven, but will settle as it cools.)

Cool before serving.

***How to Make a Pie Crust**: You can buy one at the store, but it's so easy and so much tastier if you make one instead. In a food processor, or by hand, whisk together 1¼ cups flour and ½ tsp salt. Cut 1 stick (½ cup) butter into about 10 to 12 small pieces. Pulse with flour in food processor 5 or 6 times, or cut into flour with a fork or pastry cutter to form a crumbly mixture. Add 4 Tbsp ice water, 1 Tbsp at a time, to butter and flour mixture, pulsing or mixing after each addition until dough just comes together. Wrap dough in plastic wrap and flatten slightly to form a disk. Refrigerate at least 30 minutes before rolling out and using to make a pie.

Chocolate Swirl Cheesecake Bites

I had my first taste and fell in love with these tiny bites. I guess I've had cheesecake bars before, but they weren't really finger food and somehow not as satisfying as an actual slice of cheesecake. These are the real deal. The original recipe came from a good friend who is used to professional kitchens. I experimented to make it easier, and put my own touch on the recipe. The best part: this is dessert with no plate or fork required. That's not true—the best part is how exceptional these bites taste.

INGREDIENTS

20 chocolate cream-filled sandwich cookies, finely-crushed, about 1 cup *(hint: You can make crumbs by putting cookies in a resealable baggie and beating with a rolling pin or heavy skillet.)*

2 Tbsp butter, melted (reuse bowl for melting butter to melt chocolate for easier cleanup)

2 (8-oz) packages cream cheese

½ cup sugar

1 Tbsp amaretto (can substitute 1 tsp vanilla)

½ cup sour cream

2 eggs

½ cup semi-sweet chocolate chips, melted and cooled (takes 1 minute to melt in microwave, stir after 30 seconds)

DIRECTIONS

Preheat the oven to 325 degrees.

Mix cookie crumbs with butter and press onto bottom of foil-lined 8 x 8-inch pan.

Bake for 10 minutes.

With an electric mixer, beat cream cheese, sugar, and amaretto until completely blended.

Add sour cream and mix to thoroughly combine.

Add eggs, mixing until just blended.

Stir 2 cups of batter into the melted and cooled chocolate.

Pour chocolate batter onto the crust.

Top with spoonfuls of the remaining batter.

Swirl batters with knife, being careful not to cut the crust underneath.

Bake 30 minutes or until center is mostly set.

Cool slightly and refrigerate for four hours before cutting into bite-size pieces.

Test a few, and then serve the rest.

Serves 16, easy to double using a 9 x 13-inch pan

Cookies—The Fab Four

All of these cookies sport so many fans it was impossible to pick one. Here they are in no particular order.

Oatmeal Raisin Cookies

INGREDIENTS

1 cup raisins

1 Tbsp vanilla

2 sticks butter (1 cup), softened (can be softened in microwave 8 to 10 seconds)

1 cup brown sugar

1 cup sugar

2 eggs

1½ cups flour

1 tsp baking powder

1 tsp cinnamon

1 tsp salt

3 cups old-fashioned oats (not instant oatmeal)

DIRECTIONS

Preheat the oven to 350 degrees.

Line a cookie sheet with parchment paper, or spray with cooking spray.

Combine raisins and vanilla and set aside while preparing dough.

With an electric mixer, beat butter and both sugars until light and fluffy, two to three minutes.

Beat in eggs.

Add in flour, baking powder, cinnamon, and salt, and mix until well combined.

Add raisins, vanilla, and oats, and mix until just combined.

Using a spoon, drop 2-inch mounds of dough on prepared cookie sheet.

Bake 12 to 15 minutes, until lightly browned.

Allow cookies to cool, and store in an airtight container.

Makes about 30

Best Chocolate Chip Cookies

INGREDIENTS

2 sticks butter (1 cup), softened (can be softened in microwave 8 to 10 seconds)

¾ cup sugar

¾ cup brown sugar

1½ tsp vanilla

2 eggs

2 cups flour

1 tsp baking soda

1 tsp salt

10 oz semisweet chocolate chips

DIRECTIONS

Preheat the oven to 350 degrees.

Line a cookie sheet with parchment paper or spray with cooking spray.

With an electric mixer, cream the butter and sugars.

Add the vanilla.

Mix the ingredients until they are just combined.

Add the eggs and mix lightly.

Stir in the flour, salt, and baking powder.

Fold in the chocolate chips—don't over-mix the dough.

Using a spoon, drop the cookies 2 inches apart on prepared cookie sheet.

Bake 10 to 12 minutes or until the edges are brown.

Allow cookies to cool and store in an airtight container.

Makes about 36

Honey and Lavender Icebox Cookies

INGREDIENTS

2 sticks butter (1 cup), softened (can be softened in the microwave 8 to 10 seconds)

½ cup sugar

3 Tbsp honey

2 cups flour

½ tsp salt

1 Tbsp dried lavender (can be bought online and at many grocery stores)

DIRECTIONS

With an electric mixer combine butter, sugar, and honey until light and fluffy.

Add the flour, salt, and lavender, and mix until combined.

Place one sheet of plastic wrap on a flat surface.

Place the dough on plastic wrap, using the wrap to shape the dough into a log approximately 2 inches in diameter.

Freeze thirty minutes or refrigerate 2 hours, or until firm, before baking.*

Preheat the oven to 325 degrees.

Line a cookie sheet with parchment paper or spray with cooking spray.

Slice roll of dough into ¼-inch slices.

Place slices 1 inch apart on prepared cookie sheet.

Bake 15 to 20 minutes, or until light golden brown.

Allow cookies to cool and store in an airtight container.

Makes about 48

*Dough will keep in the freezer for several weeks.

Old Fashioned Tea Cakes

INGREDIENTS

2 sticks butter (1 cup), softened (can be softened in the microwave 8 to 10 seconds)

1½ cups sugar

2 eggs

½ tsp vanilla

1 tsp baking soda

2 tsp cream of tartar

½ tsp salt

2¾ cups flour

DIRECTIONS

Preheat the oven to 350 degrees.

Line a cookie sheet with parchment paper.

With an electric mixer, cream butter and sugar until light and fluffy, 2 to 4 minutes.

Add eggs one at a time, beating well after each addition.

Add vanilla.

Beat in baking soda, cream of tartar, salt, and flour until well blended.

Drop by teaspoon onto prepared baking sheet; they will flatten as they cook, so leave at least an inch and a half between cookies.

Bake 10 to 12 minutes until light golden and barely browned on the bottom.

Allow cookies to cool and store in an airtight container.

Makes about 40

Flourless Chocolate Amaretto Cake
with Amaretto Whipped Cream

If you think you wouldn't like a flourless cake, give this one a shot, and it will change your mind. The dense chocolate taste is over the top.

INGREDIENTS

1½ sticks butter (12 Tbsp)	1 tsp vanilla
10 oz bittersweet chocolate	5 eggs
½ cup unsweetened cocoa powder	1 cup sugar
4 Tbsp amaretto liqueur	½ tsp salt

Amaretto Whipped Cream

1 cup heavy whipping cream, cold

¼ cup sugar

2 Tbsp amaretto

DIRECTIONS

Preheat the oven to 350 degrees.

Spray a 9-inch round spring-form pan or a cake pan with baking spray.

Line the bottom of the pan with parchment paper or waxed paper, and spray it again with baking spray (makes the cake much easier to remove).

Melt the butter and chocolate together in a double boiler, stirring occasionally until smooth. *(hint: You can invent a double boiler by putting a small saucepan in a larger one that is filled about ¼ of the way with water.)*

Remove from heat and allow to cool for 5 minutes.

Whisk in cocoa powder, amaretto, and vanilla.

With an electric mixer, beat the eggs, sugar, and salt on high speed for 3 to 5 minutes, until pale yellow and almost triple in volume.

Pour the chocolate mixture into the egg mixture and carefully fold them together until thoroughly combined.

Pour the batter into the prepared pan and bake for 35 to 40 minutes, until just barely set in the center.

Allow cake to cool in the pan for 30 minutes.

Invert the cake onto a flat serving plate, remove the parchment paper, and cool completely.

To make amaretto whipped cream, beat cream, sugar, and amaretto with an electric mixer at high speed until stiff peaks form. (*hint: To make cream even easier to whip, put the beaters and the cream in the freezer for a few minutes.*) (*hint: No time? Ice cream is good too!*)

Top cake and serve.

Serves 8

Frozen Lemonade Pie

Lemonade Pie makes me think of New Orleans, my favorite city next to Nashville. It's hard to compete in a city known for beignets and bread pudding, but somehow New Orleans just has the best Lemonade Pie in the world. I've sampled lots and lots, and this is my best version. There are a couple of things that would make this recipe easier (but not better), like using a premade crust or substituting the yucky thing called "dessert topping" for whipped cream. But don't do that, or you might take away the New Orleans Jazz of **Lemonade Pie**.

INGREDIENTS

Crust

6 Tbsp butter, melted

1½ cups graham cracker crumbs (about 15 crackers)
*(hint: You can buy crumbs at some grocery stores or make your
own in a food processor or in a resealable baggie using a rolling
pin or skillet to pound them.)*

2 Tbsp brown sugar

Filling

1 cup heavy whipping cream

2 tsp sugar

1 (8-oz) package cream cheese, slightly softened

1 (14-oz) can sweetened condensed milk

½ cup frozen lemonade concentrate, thawed

Juice and zest of 1 lemon

DIRECTIONS

To make the crust, preheat the oven to 350 degrees.

Mix graham cracker crumbs with butter and brown sugar and press into pie pan, packing firmly on the bottom and up the sides.

Bake for 8 minutes and then cool completely before adding filling.

To make the filling, with an electric mixer, beat the cream with the sugar until stiff peaks form.

In a separate bowl, beat together the cream cheese, condensed milk, lemonade, lemon juice, and zest until thoroughly combined.

Gently fold in whipped cream, and pour mixture on top of the crust.

Cover and refrigerate until firm, at least six hours.

Serves 8

Mini Mascarpone Cupcakes with Berry Glaze

This is the perfect little bite. No one will feel guilty about dessert!

INGREDIENTS

8 oz mascarpone cheese (about 1 cup), softened	½ tsp vanilla
2 egg whites	2½ cups flour
¼ cup vegetable oil	2 tsp baking powder
1½ cups sugar	¼ tsp salt
1 cup water	

Glaze

⅓ cup strawberries, raspberries, or blueberries (strawberries are my favorite)

2½ cups powdered sugar

DIRECTIONS

Preheat the oven to 350 degrees.

Line two mini muffin tins with paper liners.

In a large bowl, combine the mascarpone cheese, egg whites, vegetable oil, and sugar.

With an electric mixer, beat the ingredients until well combined and creamy.

Add water to combine (batter will be lumpy).

Add flour, baking powder, and salt, and mix until just combined.

Fill the mini cups to just below the rim, and bake until puffed and golden, about 18 to 20 minutes.

Remove from the oven and let cool.

Place cooled cupcakes on a wire rack or on waxed paper to glaze.

To make the glaze, purée berries in a blender or food processor.

Place the powdered sugar in a medium bowl and whisk in the fruit puree.

Top the cooled cupcakes with the berry glaze.

Let the cupcakes sit for a few minutes for the glaze to firm.

Makes 48

Peach Crisp

This is a favorite summer dessert when beautiful peaches appear in the farmers' markets, but never fear—you can happily make it in the middle of January with frozen peaches. This recipe is a little bit different because of the walnuts in the topping. They make this peach crisp really delicious.

INGREDIENTS

8 large peaches, peeled* and cut in bite-size chunks (that is about 4 cups, give or take)

1 Tbsp fresh ginger, chopped (many grocery stores sell fresh ginger in a tube that requires refrigeration)

½ cup real maple syrup

½ tsp nutmeg

Topping

¾ cup flour

¾ cup brown sugar

½ tsp salt

½ cup walnuts

6 Tbsp butter, cut in 6 pieces

DIRECTIONS

Preheat the oven to 400 degrees.

Place peaches in a deep pie pan or casserole dish sprayed with cooking spray.

Toss peaches with syrup, ginger, and nutmeg.

For the topping, add flour, brown sugar, salt, and walnuts to the bowl of a food processor (can be done by hand, but chop walnuts very finely).

Pulse until nuts are finely chopped.

Add butter and pulse until just evenly combined.

Sprinkle topping over the peaches and bake for about 40 minutes, until topping is brown and fruit is bubbling.

Serves 8

*To peel peaches, drop each one in boiling water for about 10 seconds. Remove from water, and slip off peel when cool enough to handle. Frozen peaches are ok when peaches are out of season.

Serving Suggestion: This is extra wonderful topped with vanilla ice cream.

Strawberry Shortcake

Before the days of fresh strawberries year-round in the grocery store, we had strawberries in strawberry season, which is late spring to early summer. One day we came home from Sunday school and my mother said, "Let's have Strawberry Shortcake for lunch." That was bizarre yet fabulous; whatever had spoken to her at church to urge such a decision could only be a sign of good things to come. Amen. We had strawberry shortcake outside at the picnic table. It's one of my favorite memories. I make it just the way my mother does, with a biscuit cake and fresh whipped cream. Bake up this recipe and make your own memories.

INGREDIENTS
Biscuit Cakes

3 cups flour	3 Tbsp sugar
4 tsp baking powder	1½ sticks butter (12 Tbsp), cut in ½-inch pieces
1 tsp baking soda	1 cup buttermilk
¾ tsp salt	4 Tbsp melted butter to brush baked biscuit cakes

Strawberries and Cream

2 pints strawberries, washed, hulled, and quartered (reserve 6 to 8 large ones and keep them whole for decorating the top)

¼ cup sugar

1 cup heavy whipping cream

⅓ cup powdered sugar

DIRECTIONS

Preheat the oven to 400 degrees.

Spray two cake pans with cooking spray.

Pulse dry ingredients in a food processor, or with an electric mixer, or by hand.

Add butter, and process until butter is the size of small peas.

Add buttermilk and mix quickly to barely combine.

Divide dough in half, and press each half into prepared pans.

Bake 18 to 20 minutes until lightly browned.

Cool slightly in pans.

Brush tops with melted butter.

In a bowl, combine strawberries and ¼ cup sugar, and let them sit for about 20 minutes for sugar to dissolve.

With an electric mixer, whip cream with powdered sugar at high speed until stiff peaks form, about 1 minute. *(hint: Put beater and cream in the freezer for a few minutes to make it easy to whip.)*

Place one cake on a serving platter and top with half of the sliced strawberries.

Place second layer of cake on top of the first and cover with remaining berries.

Spread whipped cream over the top and decorate with reserved whole berries.

Serves 10 to 12

The California Dessert

Weird name for a dessert, right? We were visiting a champagne cellar in Napa California, and the tour guide and I got to talking about food—imagine that. He shared a recipe for a variation of this dessert that he said he had used to impress his girlfriend enough to now be his fiancée. We like to use our own honey, so find a local honey you love! This dessert is good made with other fruit—figs and raspberries are favorites. Mascarpone can sub for ricotta in a pinch. The pepper makes it pop. California here we come!

INGREDIENTS

1 pint fresh strawberries, sliced

1 (16-oz) container whole milk ricotta cheese

4 Tbsp honey

4 Tbsp balsamic vinegar

Fresh ground pepper

1 to 2 Tbsp fresh tarragon, chopped (mint would work, but it would definitely change the flavor profile)

DIRECTIONS

For each serving, put 2 Tbsp ricotta cheese into an individual serving bowl or glass, and top with some of the strawberries.

Pour over each: 1 Tbsp honey, and 1 Tbsp balsamic vinegar.

Top with a couple of grinds of fresh-ground black pepper and a sprinkle of tarragon leaves.

Serving Suggestion: Clear glass bowls or even wide-rimmed cocktail glasses make a nice presentation, but no worries if those aren't available. The taste wins the day!

Tiramisu for Beginners

Tiramisu was the "It Girl" dessert in the 1980s, and I struggled with some fairly elaborate recipes and impossible ingredients in my tiny kitchen. That was before I discovered that a pound cake works beautifully. This dessert takes about 10 minutes to assemble and a few hours of chill time. It will probably be the most well-spent 10 minutes of your day. This is the recipe that will make you fall in love with **Tiramisu**.

INGREDIENTS

1 cup heavy whipping cream

4 oz mascarpone cheese (usually with imported cheeses at the grocery store—can substitute cream cheese)

4 Tbsp powdered sugar

½ cup strong coffee, cooled to room temperature

3 Tbsp dark rum or coffee liqueur (use what you have)

1 pound cake, plain or marbled (freezer dessert section of grocery store)

1 (8-oz) semi-sweet chocolate bar

1 Tbsp unsweetened cocoa powder

DIRECTIONS

With an electric mixer, beat cream, mascarpone cheese, and powdered sugar until combined.

Stir coffee and rum (or liqueur) together.

Cut pound cake into slices about ½-inch thick.

In an 8 x 8-inch or similar size dish (clear glass round dishes are traditional, but any casserole will work), lay half of the cake slices in a single layer.

Brush cake slices with half of the coffee mixture and cover with half of the cream mixture.

Shave about 2 Tbsp of the chocolate bar over the cream mixture, using a sharp knife or a vegetable peeler.

Repeat layer with remaining cake, coffee mixture, cream, and chocolate bar. (You can eat the rest of the chocolate bar now.)

Dust the top with cocoa powder, cover with plastic wrap, and refrigerate for 3 to 4 hours before serving, and up to 5 days.

Serves 8 to 10, easy to double

Serving Suggestion: This can be made in individual portions in cups or small glass bowls for a fancy presentation. The truth is that no one will notice how it was served once they get a bite!

Upside-Down Fruit Cobbler

Recently I got to cook dinner at a friend's vacation home, and this was the dessert I put on the menu. It's always a favorite and possibly the easiest dessert to make in the world. One of my guests was visiting in the kitchen and said she didn't waste calories on any dessert that wasn't chocolate. Well guess what, she went back for seconds. I was watching. It is that good.

INGREDIENTS

½ stick butter (4 Tbsp)

¾ cup flour

¾ cup sugar

1 tsp baking powder

¼ tsp salt

¾ cup milk

2 cups fruit (blueberries, blackberries, peaches, or a mix of all)

DIRECTIONS

Preheat the oven to 350 degrees.

Put butter in an 8 x 8-inch casserole (round pan will work too) to melt in the oven.

When butter is melted, remove the casserole from the oven.

In a mixing bowl, combine flour, sugar, baking powder, and salt.

Stir in milk to form a batter.

Pour the batter over the butter (don't stir), and top with the fruit.

Bake for approximately 50 minutes until lightly browned and fruit is bubbling.

Serve warm or at room temperature. (*hint: Delicious with a dollop of ice cream or whipped cream.*)

Serves 6 to 8, easy to double

XIII
About Setting a Table

After inviting the guests and planning a menu, setting the table can be one of the most fun aspects of throwing a party. But I have to admit that very elaborate table settings make me nervous—I'm afraid I'll break something and never be invited back. Stick to the plan of setting an attractive, comfortable, and functional table for your guests, and everyone will be happy. If the event is scheduled several days in advance and you have time to plan a table setting, then you can enjoy a little creativity. If your party is more impromptu, no one expects a perfectly-set table, and guests can pitch in to get it done. It's also nice to serve guests buffet-style from your kitchen, for a casual easy dinner that makes everyone comfortable.

The idea is to start by matching dishes to the food being served. Do you need soup bowls, a plate for salad, or just a big plate for everything? If you set a table, a tablecloth isn't a requirement, and if you do use one, it doesn't have to be an heirloom from your grandmother. My favorite one for years was a sheet with tiny flowers that I bought at Kmart. It has been washed so often you can't see the flowers anymore. Even better, our family's well-loved picnic blanket is a quilt that was my sister's college bedspread. Placemats are great and don't require a big investment. Sometimes you just want to make it fun, and cover a table with craft paper and add paper cups full of crayons. You'll be amazed by your friends' creativity!

No matter how formal or informal you go, you still need a few basics. I have a set of white plates—just plain, nothing fancy. They always work. Over the years, I've added some patterns to my collection, but you can't go wrong with a white plate. You can mix and match too. Use what you have! You need a set of flatware. It should be functional and doesn't have to be expensive. If you are serving a buffet or hosting a picnic, roll up the flatware in a napkin for easy pickup by guests. Ah napkins. There are some beautiful ones out there, but beware. If they need washing and ironing, they won't get much use. Let the occasion dictate the napkin choice. I have some nice wash-and-wear ones for entertaining, and some dish towels that double as napkins, but paper napkins belong at picnics, are easy for a casual dinner, and in truth, no one has ever refused a dinner invitation to my house because they were presented with a paper napkin—at least, not that I know of. Glassware is so abundant that you may have lots of choices. Let the event determine what you select. Unless the party is extremely formal, I think having several glasses at a place setting is just plain scary. Glasses for water and wine, if you are serving it, are perfect, and less likely to be knocked over than a large collection!

I like to make a centerpiece when I set a table, but I rarely buy flowers. We are lucky to live where lots of flowers thrive in the spring and summer, and a mix of summer flowers is hard to beat. Evergreens and interesting branches can do the trick in the winter. And never overlook the beauty of a bowl of gorgeous fruit. You don't have to invest in a collection of vases. A jar or tall glass might be just what you need. If you buy something, go for plants that can double as party favors. Potted herbs are not expensive, and are available at many groceries. Candles are nice too, and will not disappoint as an elegant centerpiece. The point is, if you have something that makes you happy, even a collection of shells or baskets, use it. That centerpiece might be the beginning of some great conversations.

Table settings should make everyone feel comfortable, including the host. If you have a delicious meal for your guests, a mismatched plate will not ruin the event. It will probably make it more charming. The main thing to remember is that it should always be a joy to entertain. That's why we do it. If you're having fun, then so are your guests!

A great way to end, The California Dessert (pg. 181)

186

Index

INDEX

INDEX

CPSIA information can be obtained
at www.ICGtesting.com
Printed in the USA
LVOW05s1955271017
554077LV00001B/1/P